MCN Days, Speedway Nights

A Reporter's Recollection of His Glory Days of Speedway

by
Andrew Edwards

Grosvenor House
Publishing Limited

This book is published by
Grosvenor House Publishing Ltd
Link House
140 The Broadway, Tolworth, Surrey, KT6 7HT.
www.grosvenorhousepublishing.co.uk

A CIP record for this book
is available from the British Library

ISBN 978-1-83975-634-4

To Joy

Foreword

By World Speedway Champion Peter Collins MBE

Unfortunately, I had lost contact with Andrew after a number of years of spending time working together on many features about a common interest and passion for our chosen sport of speedway during the 1970s and 1980s.

I managed to make contact with Andrew again very recently after he wrote a letter in the *Speedway Star* magazine, speedway's bible, backing me on a crusade I have been involved with regarding the last two promotions of Belle Vue speedway, the only club I ever raced for. Both for their refusal to recognise the club's history by issuing passes to a number of ex-Belle Vue riders, many of whom were and still are my heroes and were the reason for me developing a passion to become World Speedway Champion.

Most of these ex-riders have won British League winners medals for Belle Vue, which have become a rarity for Belle Vue in recent years.

For this reason, I have boycotted the club for the last 10 years, fighting quite a lone battle for us to get the recognition we deserve. It's surprising that many people I thought were friends have let me down in a big way. But Andrew is one of the people who has put his neck on the line publicly and spoken up for me.

Having read his letters of support for me, I decided I must contact him again and, obtaining his phone number, I gave him a call during the 2020 Covid lockdown, mainly to thank him for his support.

Surprisingly, we still had a lot in common and one thing was our love of North Wales, especially west of Conwy, including Anglesey, and the Llyn Peninsula, Abersoch, Pwllheli, Nefyn and Criccieth. Criccieth being very special as in my younger days we had many family holidays there with my parents, four brothers and sister in the 1960s, which was an impressionable time for us all. Criccieth had also been home to David Lloyd George, who was prime minister of the UK just after the First World War. Andrew told me how his love of the area began with his own parents taking him on holidays for many years to Deganwy, near Conwy when he was a boy.

I and many mates have spent many years sea fishing in the area, being owners of various seagoing boats. Also sailing many times from Conwy to the TT on the Isle of Man, and often sea fishing these waters in my fishing boat.

Andrew and I are both fortunate to have been born at the right time, just prior to our chosen sport of speedway taking off in a massive way during the 1970s and early 80s. The formation of the British League

Division One in 1965 and then British League Division Two in 1968 elevated the sport of speedway into a position of being the second most popular sport in the UK behind football. These numbers of speedway fans opened the eyes of the UK media, newspapers and TV, who all realised they needed to become part of this sport of speedway to get behind it and help push it forward after speedway had been on the back foot during the 1950s.

Speedway had seen big times before, first during the pioneering years of the late 1920s, the 1930s and, after the end of the Second World War, from the middle to late 40s.

I myself had been inspired by Peter Craven, my idol, when I started watching Belle Vue in the early 1960s. He impressed me so much and gave me a purpose in life to become World Speedway Champion. To have this burning ambition at eight years old gave me a great advantage as I was brought up on a farm in Partington, near Manchester, on my mother and father's farm. Parents who gave me great encouragement, with dad putting a pair of BSA Dandy wheels into a 1954 James Comet 98cc bike, so I could just about touch the ground, well almost. I had all the farm to go at, a cinder farmyard, grass fields and behind the farm, acres of waste land belonging to the Manchester Ship Canal Company.

I had at least a dozen school mates who also acquired motorbikes, plus my four brothers, Les, Phil, Neil and Steven, who all rode with me on the farm, most of whom became speedway and grass track riders, including Dave and Chris Morton, Dave Trownson, Wayne Hughes, Andy Reid, Steve McDermott, Geoff Rogers, Ivan Norton, George Clarke, Steve Taylor and more.

This all came about because my father, Bill, had a great interest in motorbikes, plus many of the older lads who worked for my dad rode these ex-road bikes on the farm and nearly all were stored there, and dad had a big workshop with tools and welding gear etc. and would help to keep them all going. It became a speedway farm.

My idol Peter Craven was killed at Edinburgh speedway in September 1963. I took this very badly, but nothing was going to stop me emulating my hero.

I started grass track racing at Appley Bridge, near Wigan, on 28 March 1970, four days after my 16th birthday, being taken to race meetings by my family in a Bedford Dormobile with horse trailer behind. I had a great first grass track season winning many trophies.

By 1971 I had signed for Belle Vue speedway, riding for them and also Belle Vue's nursery club Rochdale, plus still grass track racing every Sunday. I was earning in one night's racing four times more money than I could earn in one week at my job at Shell Chemicals, Carrington. By 1972, I was racing almost every night of the week, so I gave up my job at 18 years old to be a full-time racer.

This is why I said I was in the right place at the right time.

Many of the top riders were earning big money by becoming full-time speedway riders. I and many of these top riders could pay all the running costs of racing bikes and maintenance and still show a big profit at the end of each year. This had not been possible in the 1950s and 1960s. By 1976 I was World Speedway Champion and earning more than most other riders, but many were earning a good living.

During the early 1970s, I met a young Andrew Edwards, speedway correspondent for *Motor Cycle News*. Andrew came from Stourbridge in the West Midlands, having gained his speedway enthusiasm by attending speedway meetings at Cradley Heath, Wolverhampton, Birmingham with friends. These were the closest tracks to his Midlands home.

Andrew wanted to be a journalist from a very early age and to get the necessary qualifications, which at the time required a two-year course and gaining experience working for local publications and newspapers. But most of all he wanted to write about his favourite subject, speedway. This was a burning passion for him.

As speedway was now on the up and up and on the crest of a wave with the England team going it alone, because previously they had been Great Britain and included Australians and the New Zealanders in their team with Ivan Mauger, Barry Briggs and Ronnie Moore.

Now England were good enough to go it alone as England. I was in the team when we won the World Cup at Wembley in 1973, Katowice, Poland in 1974 and Norden, Germany in 1975. I scored 12-point maximums in all three of these World Finals and I was European Champion, winning at Wembley in 1974 and World Champion in 1976.

By this time all the major newspapers had a speedway reporter who attended all the major speedway finals with all expenses paid. Usually, they travelled on the same flights as riders and officials, plus TV. This is the extraordinary list from those times: London Weekend ITV, Dave Lanning; BBC radio, Tony Millard; BBC Radio Manchester, Dick Bott, alias Dick Julian, Jack Elder, Richard Kennedy who were reporters for *Daily Mail*, *Daily Mirror*, *Daily Express*, *Sunday Express* and *Daily Star*. *Daily Mail*, Keir Radnedge; *Daily Star*, Mike Beale; *Daily Mirror*, Graham Baker; *Daily Mirror North*, John Edgeley; *Speedway Star* and *Daily Express*, Southern edition, Phillip Rising; *The Sun*, Dave Lanning; *Manchester Evening News*, Richard Frost, David Burke, John Turner, Phil Jones; Piccadilly Radio and Key 103, John Pickford; *Sunday Mirror* (who sponsored the World Championship), Keith Fisher and Don Clarke; *Express and Star*, Wolverhampton Tom Johnson; *Speedway Mail*, Tony McDonald; *Speedway Star*, Martin Rogers.

The main players amongst those names formed SWAPA (Speedway Riders and Photographers Association) in 1978 in Landshut, Germany after the World Team Cup Final. Among the speedway photographers in those days were Alf Weedon, Mike

Patrick, John Hipkiss, Wright Wood, Trevor Meeks, and Mike Kilby.

When I won my World Championship in Katowice, Poland in 1976, I was on the front and back pages of the *Daily Mirror* which is unheard of today.

When I said that Andrew was in the right place at the right time, this is how he became the main speedway reporter for *Motor Cycle News*, his dream job.

By 1973, Peter Strong was the editor of *MCN* and also doing the speedway for the paper. In September 1973, Peter advertised the job of speedway reporter for *MCN*. Andrew applied and was soon walking into the job, the perfect man for it. At the time, Andrew had been doing speedway reports for his local paper, the *County Express* where he worked, plus the *Sunday Mercury* and sending speedway results to all the daily national newspapers that wanted them.

Of course, I met Andrew very soon after his appointment, got on very well, and every magical speedway moment I achieved, I shared with Andrew as he was always there during the peak of my career.

These times were always very sociable as we often stayed in the same hotel before many World Championship events all over the world and I and my mechanics flew to Los Angeles from London for the 1982 World Final at the LA Coliseum, Andrew was sitting with our group on the Boeing 747 jumbo on the flight. We always knew Andrew would report on the events very well and he was always trusted to say the right things in the reports.

It was always great to know that when I received my *Motor Cycle News*, he always did me and the sport proud. Such a pleasure to read what he had written. I think that all of the other riders felt the same.

I always felt that Andrew had become part of my team, and I am sure many other riders felt the same.

I'm sure that Andrew really enjoyed his dream job. He was part of the whole experience during the best times of our lives. He also reported on some of the biggest grass tracks ever held on the planet, along with *MCN* grass track reporter John Simcock. The biggest one being at Hereford in 1976, which I managed to win.

It was all good times for Andrew and I, and I always made time for him.

I felt very honoured when Andrew asked me to write the Foreword for this book and said yes immediately.

I wish him all the success in the world regarding sales of this very interesting book.

It was fantastic that we were both there.

Good luck,

Peter Collins, MBE.

Acknowledgements

I would like to thank *Motor Cycle News*, the prestige motorcycling weekly newspaper for permission to use some of the features and stories I wrote for them which I found in their wonderful bound volumes at head office, and for the unstinting work on my behalf by Ali in particular, in being so patient with my inquiries and for finding information I could not. To Mike Patrick and John Hipkiss, whose photos are now owned by John Somerville and John Hall, Alf Weedon and the *County Express*, who I hope are happy with my inclusion of the Stourbridge Institute badminton team from all those years ago. To Joy for encouraging me over several years to finish my book. All errors are mine and mine alone.

Introduction

This is not meant as a history of speedway or motorcycle sport, those topics have already been ably told many times by greater pundits and writers than I, but my own story, in my own words and using my memories.

My story attempts to give a glimpse of thoughts and reminiscences of the sporting side of motorcycle sport from my involvement during the years I was employed by the greatest biking weekly newspaper of all time, *Motor Cycle News*.

I feel highly honoured to have been part of their editorial team for well over 20 years, years which saw many changes at the flagship EMAP (East Midland Allied Press) newspaper, some good, some not so good. As I said, this is my story.

The day I went to an interview as a rookie reporter in 1973 and was given the job by editor Peter Strong changed my life forever.

It began a whirlwind career, meeting, becoming friends with many of the sport's great riders of the time and seeing at first hand and giving our over 100,000 readers on a weekly basis, reports of all of motorcycling's great stories of the day, week in, week out, from whatever part of the world they took part in. *MCN* was there, or had contacts and "stringers", dozens of local journalists and bike sport enthusiasts, who would tell us what was going on, old-style news gathering which I was brought up on from age 17 working in local newspapers.

We were unequivocally *Sun*-style with banner headlines, short, to-the-point stories, as much razzamatazz as you could get in a newspaper. We led the market in a brash and brazen sort of way, some liked us for it and some always hated it or said they did. But I know they read it.

But we were always after that next big scoop, and there were plenty of them from the hardworking band of informed reporters, in road racing, scrambles (motocross), speedway, grass track, trials, drag racing, anything which was raced on two wheels, who searched worldwide for the best stories supported by the best photographs, with the banner "exclusive" written big as often as possible. I played my small part in the production of that *MCN* institution which was highly successful in marketing terms for year after year. It was an unprecedented success.

The blue *MCN* goggles logo was famous worldwide as a top-rated franchise, and fearlessly *MCN*, never one to stand still, changed its very popular blue merchandise to an even brighter, brasher red and yellow. Just wearing my "staffer" *MCN* logo-embroidered jacket got me into meetings in Germany where nobody else in the press corps got in easily to do their job! Just because I was there, representing *MCN*! Very impressive.

MCN sent me all over the country and the world, covering top international speedway, long track and ice speedway, and I hope that I increased its popularity in an era in which for many years, Britain was top of the crop. It was an unbelievable, jaw-dropping experience to have been given the opportunity of world travel, and seeing more speedway meetings than practically anyone, other than the riders themselves, in my dream job, for 25 years.

I explore my roots in provincial journalism before *MCN* and a snapshot of the wonderful hot metal printing industry onto the birth of computer publishing, freelancing, public relations, and later even a spell of court reporting.

This is my personal passage through a major part of my sports writer's life. Welcome to that dream.

Contents

Chapter 1	The wrong car park	1
Chapter 2	World Final Poland	4
Chapter 3	My early days	11
Chapter 4	My dream	17
Chapter 5	Brierley Hill office	23
Chapter 6	Tragedy on track	28
Chapter 7	Four meetings in four days, one in Poland!	31
Chapter 8	Second phase, *MCN*	38
Chapter 9	Early *MCN* days	46
Chapter 10	*MCN* office for japes	66
Chapter 11	*MCN* story	80
Chapter 12	Peter Arnold nostalgia	104
Chapter 13	Fan to speedway reporter	109
Chapter 14	*MCN* on tour, to Silverstone GP	119
Chapter 15	Back to the speedway	124
Chapter 16	Cradley days	133
Chapter 17	Tragedy off track	139
Chapter 18	*MCN* Golden Helmet days	148
Chapter 19	*MCN* state of our sport!	162
Chapter 20	The press corps, Simon Wigg	169
Chapter 21	F1!	182

Chapter 22	The TT	189
Chapter 23	Back to speedway. Again	197
Chapter 24	Speedway GPs take over	208
Chapter 25	*EastEnders*!	217
Chapter 26	Honda speedway engine	229
Chapter 27	*MCN* stars of four decades	233
Chapter 28	More *MCN* changes	237
Chapter 29	My era 1973–98	246
Chapter 30	Life After *MCN*	251
Chapter 31	In court!	255
Chapter 32	Speedway freelance years	263
Chapter 33	Vintage speedway	274
Chapter 34	Programmes	283
Chapter 35	Characters along the way	286
Chapter 36	Mum's book	302
Chapter 37	The biggest laugh	306

Chapter 1

The wrong car park

I'd parked in the wrong car park, of course. It was a lovely June day in 2015, and I was paying my first visit to *Motor Cycle News*'s Peterborough offices as *MCN* had kindly said I could look at their files to help me continue researching my memoir, my life reporting on motorcycle sport, mainly speedway, for over 20 years between 1973–1996.

When I'd extricated my car from the car park to the proper Bauer publishing car park, I got my visitor's badge from reception – this too was a first for me too, unlike any *MCN* offices I'd ever worked in – and Ali, the editor's secretary, gave me access to a desk and the stern-looking musty, dark black, *MCN* bound yearly copies, from "steam radio" times in 1955 to the present.

I was given a cardboard box containing most of the *MCN* index books, many tatty with age, as was the cardboard box, some pages missing, some hardly hanging together at all, and amusingly, a couple of sweet wrappers and a packet of coloured bike helmet ear plugs, and a small brown leatherette index book in quite good condition.

What I saw on the cover were the words "1979–81". It was my own untidy, squiggly handwriting staring back at me. First time I'd seen it for 34 years. It gave me an extraordinary cold shiver down my spine, and I'm sure the hairs on the back of my neck were standing up. Those simple, clumsily written numbers in my own hand brought home what I was looking at. My own madeleine moment when your own life comes into sharp memory and focus. What I was about to delve into through the index books, the bound copies of *MCN* contained not only everything I'd ever written for the biggest selling motorcycle newspaper in the world, but they also included, bound up too, my life, or a big slice of my life. For wrapped in those dusty old, beautiful bound copies of *MCN* was the life I had lived, the life I'd lived among motorcycle sport giants of journalism and two-wheeled heroes at *MCN*.

"They", my friends and acquaintances, said I'd got my dream job. Damn right I had, and I knew it. I was the luckiest person in the world.

After retirement, I decided to write my story, mainly relating to *MCN* as I'd been there, man and boy, from 1973–1996, and what happened after those days too. It was to be a reflection of my thoughts, my memories, to relive a great time in my life.

I'd started writing the book 12 months earlier than my *MCN* Peterborough visit. I'd written just over 31,000 words and I was proud of myself. A 200-word lead story or a 1,000-word feature was what I'd done all my reporting life. Proud, until I met my old colleague Peter Oakes, the legendary journalist who had agreed to read what I'd written. Peter said hello in the Oundle Waitrose café, halfway between our two homes, and straightaway said, "I've got a big shock for you, you've only written enough for about 66 pages of a book, that's all, it's not enough." I was mortified, although I tried at least to look calm. I knew the book was not finished by a very long way, but my resolve at that moment started to wobble. How do authors do it? How do they write so many words? It was back to the drawing board for me, as I trusted Peter implicitly in his judgement, with his experience of national newspaper journalism and speedway book publishing. So that's how I began again, a big re-think of how I could possibly tell my own life story. The journey had begun again.

Chapter 2
World Final Poland

Fast-forward to a balmy September day in Poland in 1976, surrounded by 120,000 speedway fans and Peter Collins, a true Brit, my friend, wins the World Speedway Championship Final, the first Englishman to do so for 14 years. And I'm there to report the event for my paper, *Motor Cycle News*.

It was one of the golden ages for British speedway and one which I was able to see at first hand, meeting and getting to know some really wonderful characters and friends along the way and now, many, many years later, looking back with fondness and nostalgia at an era which may possibly never be emulated again.

Wow, reporting speedway worldwide for *Motor Cycle News*, life cannot get much better than this, I thought. One of very few individuals to have a full-time job reporting speedway, my own passion; I realise that I was very lucky to be in this unique position.

But my speedway story started much earlier, when I first saw the sport at the Black Country stadium at Dudley Wood, the proud spartan home of Provincial League Cradley Heath, in the West Midlands, often the wooden spoonists rather than champions. But how all that was to change many years later!

In 1960, at the age of 15, I saw Cradley reborn after starting in 1947 before closing down in 1952. I can't say I was at the first meeting on Saturday, 16 April 1960 against Rayleigh, but attend I did that first season. I was a pillion passenger on a friend's 200cc Zundapp Bella scooter, which had an electric starter, unusual for those days. It was a beauty, or so I thought at the time! In 1961, we ventured to Coventry speedway to see the "big boys" in the National League – Cradley were in the "second division" of racing in the newly formed brash Provincial League.

We missed the first six heats of the Central Challenge match against Swindon because we got lost, not knowing our way to Coventry's Brandon track! I still have the programme from that match, but have no memory of the racing, except to say we stood too close on the third bend and got covered in shale! So that was why nobody was standing quite so close! Doh! And that's why people laughed at us "rookies" to speedway! I see from the programme (6d) that it was Coventry's 14th season, and we attended the 23rd match of that year which was won by the Bees 48–30 and the team manager, Bob Mark, was pictured on the front cover, not one of his riders, who included Kazim Bentke, Ron Mountford, Nigel Boocock, Les Owen, Jack Young, Jim Lightfoot and Nick Nicholls, while Teo Teodorowicz was Robin's number one.

I do have better memories from 1963 with Provincial League champions Wolverhampton at Monmore Green, taking on the legendary National League team from Norwich on Friday, October 11, which included superstar and then four-times world champion Ove Fundin, the first time I ever saw him ride. Fundin, unbeaten in his first three rides, was then sensationally beaten in his fourth by Wolves' own favourite Maurie Mattingley, his first win of the night. There was uproar in the stadium, and I don't think Ove took defeat well! It was a humdinger of a meeting, in front of a very full house, and despite a second win by Wolves Tommy Sweetman in the final heat 13, a second place from Norwich's Reg Trott meant a Wolves 3–2 win, no other finishers, but a 38–39 "away" win for the Stars. I still have that programme in my collection. Little did I know I would meet Ove many years later. And "Little Boy Blue" Nigel Boocock.

A Cradley Heath training school had been run in the winter to find new members of the Heathens' team for the new, untried 1960 Provincial League, organised mainly by ex-Heathens' rider, Phil Malpass. This was a happy revival time for the Heathens.

Those formative years, both for me as a wide-eyed spectator, and the Provincial League teams between 1960–64 were simply brilliant. In 1964 PL speedway went "black", running without permissions from the bike race authorities, but still made a healthy go of it. This led to common sense returning the following year with the formation of the British League when the

PL promoters were linked up with the few remaining, ailing National League teams to form one big, successful league, which went on to achieve much greater interest and coverage nationwide and which was the cornerstone of British speedway's successful, what I call golden years, for the sport. Although many older fans would say the same for the immediate post-war speedway years.

My early visits to Cradley from my home just down the road in Amblecote were by bus, then by scooter. I blush at the thought of the light blue Triumph Tina automatic, possibly the worst bike ever made by Triumph, on which I passed my test and which was later stolen, although unfortunately recovered. The automatic clutch on mine broke, and I refabricated some new metal from a bean can to hold the spring back in. The spring, about six inches long, was very strong and I had the bike on its side in the garden trying to push this spring back on by hand before trying to get a couple of screws back on the outer plate. Several times I had to let it go and the spring would shoot upwards into the sky, past my nose, until I just managed on another attempt to screw it up before this happened again. Phew. Later, I had proper Honda motorcycles, followed by a £50, rotten as a pear Austin A30, registration OUY 830, with very little in the way of brakes. The sills had rotted away when I bought it, and I stuffed newspapers in them before glass fibre finished the job. My elder brother Dave, who had a Mini, wouldn't get in it! Things were different in those days; not so much traffic for one thing! The A30,

I remember, did get me to places like Belle Vue speedway, Manchester, for the first time and never broke down, even taking me on holiday to North Wales, again without a hitch. Looking back, it was probably a minor miracle the old thing made it. Must have been a decent, if slow, engine though.

But in speedway we all had our heroes, and my boyhood hero was Ivor Brown in those early days of Cradley's "second period" between 1960–1995. Cradley had operated earlier, from buoyant 1947 when war-weary sport-deprived people clamoured back to the speedways. This euphoria didn't last, with Cradley's closure in 1952, when speedway was beginning to struggle for teams and big crowds.

If it had not been for the on-track performances of number one Brown in the swinging sixties, Cradley would have sunk even lower than they were already. They were a Cinderella club, often trying to avoid the wooden spoon for last place year after year. That was the underlying beauty of speedway in those formative years. Nobody who turned up knew exactly what was going to happen. A home victory, a draw, a home defeat, all results were on the cards for season after season. The unpredictability of the racing was what made is so special for so many thousands of fans. Today if a team continually loses, the fans drift away. In those days Cradley certainly bucked the trend. Full, and I mean full, terraces, year after unsuccessful year.

The Heathens as I said were not a league winning side and just to win at home was great, and yet the fans turned up week after week for the speedway fever they had, fed by some of the best racing ever seen in Britain. The track at Dudley Wood was supposedly shaped like Wembley and the same size. It certainly did not frighten any visiting team rider, unlike the Exeter County Ground with its steel safety fence made from World War Two shelters. Racing was always fair, and all riders tried their best in a rough and tumble league at first. But it was Brown who was the mainstay of the Heathens from 1961–68.

He was always immaculately attired in his trademark white rugby style jumper underneath his green and white CH body colour, shiny black leathers, gleaming silver machine under the lights, green and white socks rolled over on top of his boots, round throttle guard on the right handlebar, and the best starter in the league. Brown supposedly used the best, most expensive clutches in the business from grass tracker George Bewley and always had immaculate bikes.

That is one magic that has disappeared as modern machines have changed into multi-coloured advertising hoardings. Brown used his great equipment to good effect too. He often jumped into the lead at the first bend and clung to that white line as if he was glued to it. Boring? Not really, if he was your man, the man who Cradley could rely on, the main points machine for the Heathens, and without his hundreds of points, Cradley would have struggled even more away from home. And he was by no means speedway's only "white liner".

He was one of the first superstars of the Provincial League and never looked back after signing for the Black Country team from Great Yarmouth. He could beat the best on a weekly basis, and his duels with the top riders from the old enemy "up the road" at Wolverhampton became legendary in the Midlands.

Brown began his league career with Leicester Hunters (1953–59) and riding for Yarmouth Bloaters (1958–60) before reaching the pinnacle of his career as a Heathen. With him, Cradley won the Knockout Cup in 1961 and 1963 and had many victories in the league's premier match race competition, called the Silver Sash in 1961–62–63. He was almost always a ten-point average man or thereabouts, but in 1965 he had a career-changing crash at the massive Internationale individual meeting at Wimbledon, tangling badly with Ove Fundin. Fundin was never forgiven by Cradley folk. Brown received severe lower spine injuries, yet he came back and soldiered on till 1968 when he retired, never being quite the old Ivor. He died aged 77 in 2005. He was the postmaster in his home village of Wymeswold, Leicestershire. A great stalwart for Cradley Heath. Every book has got to have a "stalwart" in it, so here it is! "Brownie" was a stalwart.

Chapter 3

My early days

I was born at home in Amblecote, near Stourbridge, West Midlands, one of the country's great crystal glass making industrial towns, the second son of Stan and Mary. My elder brother Dave went to work in Africa, where he met his wife, Christine, later having many homes together in Australia, moving from Perth, Sydney, Queensland and Tasmania. In 1998 my partner, Joy, and I had a wonderful time visiting them in Tasmania, which we loved. Dave is an open-air man and his love of the mountains took him to North Wales most weekends, and sometimes I'd accompany him and his mates although I was seven years younger than him. We also had a lovely touring holiday in Scotland, many years before the motorways extended all the way north, in my cousin Jack's Triumph Herald, who did all the driving. We spilled a bottle of milk in the car and if you've ever done that, you'll know that you never get rid of the putrid smell, despite much scrubbing. So, our tour was accompanied by a rancid milk aroma. Brother Dave did his two years national service in the Royal Navy on minesweepers working in communications.

My mother's dad, Billy Hicks, was a skilled glassmaker (Stourbridge being a hot bed of that industry as I've said) and worked for Thomas Webb and Sons for 47 years, retiring in 1949. He had lost his wife early on and lived with Mom and Dad all their married life, cared for by my saint of a mother until he died at a ripe old contented age.

Dad was in the steel industry and worked for Bayliss Jones and Bayliss in Wolverhampton, which meant he was in a reserved occupation when the Second World War started and served in the auxiliary fire service and witnessed much of the horrible heavy bombing by the Germans in the Midlands; Birmingham and Coventry not being far away. But he was fairly reticent in recalling too many events. I remember one incident though, when the fire service attended a fire in a building which was evacuating very quickly as a bomb that had not gone off was stuck upright in the middle of a room, looking like an old-fashioned stovepipe, but much more deadly!

When she was little, Mom had to look after her dad and even took his cooked dinner to him from home in Wollaston, near Stourbridge, at lunchtime to his Amblecote works, wrapped up in a cloth, day after day, running all the way! Woe betide if it was cold.

Runaway lorry, driver jumped out, smashed a telegraph
pole, letterbox, our brick wall and nearly our house in
Amblecote. I was in a bedroom, sleeping, top left.

Mom and Dad were mad on sport, especially tennis
and would do anything for a game. I caught the bug
and loved tennis and then later, badminton. They were
also mad keen cyclists and went everywhere by bicycle.
Dad did not take his car test until he was 50, buying his
first car, an already old Morris Eight belonging to
Uncle Peter, after Mom became more and more reliant
on transport because of serious health problems,
which unfortunately bugged her for the rest of her life.
But she was a fighter was my mom and would never
give in. She was the boss in most things in the house.
She even had a spell when, given nothing more than a
set of teaching aids and notes, she taught at a local
private school and stood in front of young children
giving them their basic education. This must have
been very daunting as this was a woman whose

education was only rudimentary at most. Those were the days! We were probably the last in our street to have a television and always trooped next door to watch the Cup Final for years and years. With mum's extra money from teaching, I remember she purchased our first TV set, dazzling black and white of course!

Mom took a lively interest in all the results of the speedway because I was so keen, and my parents were both supportive in everything my brother and I ever achieved and tried to cajole us both into getting as much education we could, without undue strain being put upon us. It worked for my brother, who went to university and got his degree and master's degree. I got as far as the same grammar school eventually, as he did, passing the then 13 plus exam, but only got as far as a sixth form called 6C – for commercial stream – where non-academics like us did not take exams as we were not clever enough for A levels. Doh!

But it did me good because the editor's secretary gave us lessons in typewriting and shorthand which were to become very helpful for my career in journalism. Academic qualifications were not for me, but many teachers did educate us about life and gave up their time willingly. One I remember taught me not only the rudiments of classical music, but of jazz too and we got to listen to his vinyl records of drummer Gene Krupa, great trumpeter Louis Armstrong and many, many others, which left me with a great lifetime love of all sorts of music. Especially rock and blues. I was so happy to go to the early 1960s blues shows in

Birmingham which came over from America, when I saw legendary artists such as Sonny Boy Williamson, Howling Wolf, Buddy Guy, Sonny Terry and Brownie McGhee, even Sleepy John Estes! Who? Plus the Count Basie, Duke Ellington big bands several times, the Buddy Rich big band, most of the trad bands before the Beatles, top folkies, plus Brenda Lee and Melanie. And plenty more. What a musical education I had. The best era ever for music, through the 60s, 70s and 80s.

I always said the best day of my life was the day I left school, but I don't suppose schooldays were too bad, looking back overall! Except for two school bullies, who were both teachers.

One "old boy" you might have heard of was Robert Plant, the lead singer of legendary rock group Led Zeppelin, who was a local boy and was a "grammar grub" as we were all called locally. He, I believe, was expelled, but that didn't seem to upset his life's aspirations. I have a photograph of the entire Stourbridge King Edward VI grammar school taken in 1963, me at one end and Robert at the other.

My friend Gareth Morgan was a "friend" of Robert's in Stourbridge but being a pupil of the Bluecoat school in the town, they were enemies and rivals for the affections of the local girls, and Gareth remembers chasing or being chased up Stourbridge High Street with some "argument" over a girl. Gareth also saw Robert's first gig, somewhere at the back of the bus garage in the town, where he remembers a very, very young Robert being booed off stage because at that stage he could not play or sing, according to Gareth. For many years, Gareth still saw Robert in the area as Robert still has local connections nearby and is often seen in local music pubs. Sadly, Gareth died, before his time, of the ghastly Covid pandemic in 2021.

When I told my partner, Joy, a lifelong fan of Led Zeppelin who had a collection of the group's records on vinyl, which are still played, that I'd gone to the same school as Robert, she didn't believe me for a long while! Thought I was pulling her leg.

Chapter 4
My dream

I always wanted to be a reporter, don't know why, but I always loved words, books, motoring and motorcycle magazines, and Mom was an avid reader of everything, and through her working in the binding department of stationers and booksellers Mark and Moody in Stourbridge knew Eric Bull, one of the *County Express* reporters, who came to the house once, I remember, to tell me about the job. The *County Express* was the local weekly newspaper, which everyone had. I think she hoped Eric would put me off, but he didn't. Luckily.

My brother went from job to job, never settling down to a profession, unable to find his niche. He was in banking for a while and worked at a Birmingham branch. One day he forgot the keys to the bank and Mom had to get on another bus to take the keys to him before the bank could open.

Before his national service, Dave used to drive us mad when he was learning Morse code, which he listened to on shortwave on the big old radio in the house! I think he had some quite wild times with his fellow "oiks" in the Navy, one of which involved the repatriation of a barrel of beer from a pub, which got them in big, big trouble with the navy chiefs.

But after university and plenty of studying, he carved out a career in teaching. One of his early jobs in Africa was teaching electronics to Zambian police officers.

But back to the start of my working life. In 1963, I realised the dream I always had, to become a journalist. Straight from King Edward VI Grammar School, Stourbridge, West Midlands. I failed my 11 plus exam. My life supposedly was not going to be among the academics, but among the "others" in secondary modern education, which I also enjoyed for two years. Not for me the Ivory Towers of Oxford! I settled in well I thought at Longlands school. That was after a happy start at Enville Street Junior School. I recall I was in some play or other, but got stage fright, which meant I missed out dozens of pages of dialogue, and so the production had no meaning at all. It was my first and last time treading the "boards". Thank goodness. But at Longlands, I passed my "second chance" 13 plus and got to the grammar school, despite awful maths knowledge, which remains with me to this day. My non-academic success was not a good start to looking for a job, with O level passes in English Language and English Literature (I somehow took Literature twice and passed it again), and, I believe, Geography for some reason; I must have liked the teacher.

But Colonel Moody (they kept their rank in peacetime in those days, sadly, and Lieutenant Colonel

O'Mara was a sub-editor too) was the *County Express* proprietor of the family weekly newspaper group in my own hometown and gave me a job as a junior reporter, and years of tea making began. I still have Col Moody's handwritten letter offering me the job of junior reporter. Little did he know what opportunities he had opened up for me with his generous offer of a job.

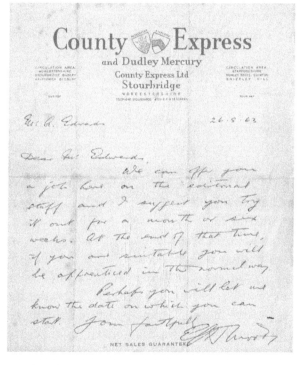

Letter handwritten by *County Express* owner Col. Moody offering me a job on his newspaper in Stourbridge 1963

My reporting career meant further education. I see from a little postcard I still have from the National

Council for the Training of Journalists in 1965 I was given a "pass" in second year English and law. That was achieved in a two-year one day a week block release course in Birmingham. I would have probably learnt even more (including how to take a high-speed shorthand note) if I had gone more often, but the calls of the Second City were great, and the films were inviting for an afternoon absentee junior reporter. One of my lecturers in current affairs at the journalists' college was Coventry MP Leslie Huckfield, who helped Triumph set up the workers' co-operative which ran the famous motorcycle manufacturer after the Meriden strike in 1973.

I knew little of real life, the stuffy old grammar school being boys only for a start but learnt at the sharp end quite quickly in the Stourbridge office under the orders of chief reporter Jack Haden, who went everywhere by bike wearing his bottle glasses and cycle clips on his suit trousers and was a great and respected historian for the area. It was a daily learning curve of adding weekly cuttings into mouldering old yellow files of the local great and the good to await later use in their obituaries! Tedious. Then the rounds of magistrates' courts, council meetings, daily police calls, fires, even being the amateur dramatic critic, for which I was phenomenally ill equipped. Followed by typing up on mechanical machines (no computers) of wedding reports which were sent in by the families to go in the newspaper practically word for word with an intro put on by me. Golden weddings! The bane of my life. Everyone seemed to achieve 50 years of wedded bliss, or even the diamond wedding congratulations of 60 years, and it was my job to knock on the door of the sweet old couple and get their life story off them for an article in next week's paper. It was very hard work sometimes to say anything about them which was colourful and meaningful "copy" for the paper.

But it quickly helped my interviewing "technique".

In those far-off days, big funerals of the mighty, rich or just lucky, were covered in full by local papers and the *County Express* was no different. It meant going to the church with notebook in hand and asking for the names of the mourners as they filed into church. If you missed anyone, or even worse, got their name wrong when it appeared in next week's report of the funeral, you were in big trouble from the family and the editor. That was how I learned to be accurate with people's names, most times, so that sets me up to fail in this book!

I remember I arrived too late at one really big funeral in Pensnett, and all the mourners were already in church. Trying to be resourceful and not receive a big telling off, I corralled them all, standing in the doorway as they all came out of church, hundreds of them, and asked their names! I think I must have got away with that one!

Sometimes, local reporters, me included, did stories on the quiet for the evening paper, the *Express and Star*, based in Wolverhampton. It was a good little earner, especially if they wanted a report from a local funeral with mourners' names as we were paid what in those days was called "linage", stories paid for by the line, so more names, more money on the side for me to go with my wage, paid in cash in a little brown envelope.

Chapter 5
Brierley Hill office

After a while, I was assigned by the *County Express* to the district office in Brierley Hill, where the chief reporter was Phil Malpass, who happily for me was the former Cradley Heath speedway captain. He had held a unique position in the sport as he continued with a career in journalism along with a parallel career, speedway riding. He took his holiday entitlement in days off for the away matches. It was from him I learnt many of the stories of the first days of the Heathens from 1947 when he turned out for the team, eventually becoming their captain.

Many a happy hour was to be had reading old programmes and magazines found in the office and listening to Phil's old tales. During this time, Phil and I produced a five-part history of Cradley speedway. He wrote the majority of his memories of the old days when he was centrally involved, and I brought the history up to date before it was all published by the *County Express* in 1970.

There were several iconic photos used in that series, one of which was probably the earliest action photo from that first year in 1947 when there were no floodlights, meetings being held in the afternoon, with no Lukes' football pitch in the middle. I believe it could have been the first match against Wombwell, which was said to have attracted 17,000 people. There was an early photo of the site when it had showmen living in gypsy-style caravans in their winter quarters. Plus, we published the only photo ever taken of the great Australian international Graham Warren wearing the CH colours of Cradley in the only match he ever rode for the Heathens (at Tamworth) before controversially signed by the Birmingham promoters, who also ran Cradley, much to the great annoyance of Heathens fans.

As I already had an interest and a little knowledge of speedway, my embryonic speedway reporting began with sprawling columns in the local paper of each Saturday night match. Saturday evenings became lucrative later when I covered the Cradley league meetings for the *Sunday Mercury*, who had a lively interest in the sport. That gave me my first experience of having to write up the meeting very quickly at the end of a meeting, to phone "copy" minutes after the final wheel had turned in time for the deadline to get the report into the next day's *Mercury*. Before that, I had days to tweak my report for the *County Express*, a weekly paper. That was my jolly life for seven years.

I was able to make more pin money as in those days national newspapers, some even as far as Scotland, wanted results from league matches phoned in immediately after the meetings, which I did directly from the track. Getting the use of a phone was a big issue at the track in those days, no mobile phones, remember! Having to fight for first use of the only phone, begrudgingly provided by the speedway office staff, with the local freelance, who just came to the stadium for the result and quizzed me if anything of note had happened. Cheeky.

I still believe, even after all these years, after seeing speedway right up to the modern day, that those early years for me, particularly the 1960–61 seasons of the unpredictable antics of the Provincial League, which helped in no small measure to save speedway from possible annihilation, was the most exciting speedway I ever saw. You never knew what was going to happen next. It was its lovely character that was at the very heart of great entertainment. We need plenty more of that now for the sport to survive.

There were terrific characters. The late Chris Julian was so harum-scarum, he was known to knock his own team mates off on the last bend of a race at Cradley with his over-exuberant riding of his bucking machine. Years later, Julian, after a lifetime of dangerous speedway racing, died as a result of a gyrocopter crash. You were hooked in week after week as a fan. For instance, it would be announced at Cradley that Swindon Robins were to be the visitors next week, so you had to go because it was your only chance that season of seeing their star number one, the legendary Barry Briggs. The week after that it was Exeter Falcons, so it was your only chance of seeing the great Ivan

Mauger, their star rider. And so on, week in, week out. It was unmissable stuff. The crowds loved it and came in their thousands. There were enough teams then to run a full league season without having to resort to two visits of each team in A and B fixtures, so the weekly "fix" was always fresh and new.

In 1964 the Provincial League ran "black" outside speedway's controlling body. It still made no difference. Entertainment was the name of the game and everyone still loved it. It was the upstart PL promoters who helped make our sport so lively. The likes of larger-than-life businessmen Mike Parker and Reg Fearman and many more new promoters who saved the day and improved the product for us on the terraces. In 1965 the Provincial League was reinstated, amalgamating with the big boys in the British League and it grew into a bigger sport, with terrific entertainment, and a new second division and even more tracks for supporters to support.

I went with my friends Brian and Robert not only to home matches on Saturdays, but to as many away meetings with Cradley as we could. Highlights were visits to Sheffield, Swindon, and my favourite of the entire speedway year, a trip down to Exeter when the Heathens took on their frightening, steel-panelled safety fence, high-speed banked track, round the local rugby field. Thinking about it all these years later still gives me a thrill.

I had gone from scooters, bikes, to the ownership of an almost top-of-the-range Ford Escort 1300E (bright banana yellow it was), and I remember Brian, a very good driver, drove it back from Exeter to Birmingham in an hour and a half, cruising at 90mph. No traffic at midnight on the M5 and no speed cameras. Amazing. You'd have no driving licence left now with all those speed cameras zapping away.

Wherever we went, we got to know the best route to all the tracks we visited, where the best pub was and not least, the best chip shop. I particularly remember a fine chippy just outside Halifax after visiting the Dukes fixtures at The Shay with the Heathens for many seasons.

Chapter 6

Tragedy on track

In among the superbly happy memories of my early speedway life comes a terrible memory, when the sport lived up to the advert placed in every speedway programme. "Motor sports are dangerous." The first death of a rider that I saw was that of 26-year-old Welshman Ivor Hughes, the Cradley Heath rider who crashed at Dudley Wood on 20 August 1966.

Ivor was a young man who had come through the ranks at Cradley, watched by his adoring fans, from a struggling reserve through a great improvement in his abilities which had seen him rise to become one of the stars of the team, especially when he invested in a new ESO engine, which later became the Jawa, and suited his style admirably, more so than the JAP.

But his star did not burn bright enough or long enough. He was cut down before he achieved what I am sure would have been greatness in the sport.

This is shown by looking back on an international challenge match Cradley had against Sweden's Vargarna club on August 6 that year. Ivor had got 10 brilliant points against the strong touring side, including two victories to top the score chart, which included Ivor Brown and Colin Pratt, who got eight points each.

In the second half final, Ivor had one of his finest victories, defeating current world champion Bjorn Knutson, which had his Midland club fans jumping for joy and calling out his name from the terraces – "Ivor, Ivor, Ivor."

Not this time meaning Ivor Brown, that great number one of the CH club, but up-and-coming and inspiring youngster, Ivor Hughes.

Up to that night on 6 August, Ivor Hughes was rated as the club's number two in the averages, beating names like Brown, Howard Cole, Chum Taylor and Clive Featherby to that honour. Ivor had just scored an unbeaten tally in a World Championship round too.

On that fateful night of 20 August, my friends and I stood on the exit of turn one and had seen Ivor remain unbeaten against Sheffield in a British League match. But in the second half, Ivor was involved in a crash on that bend with two Sheffield riders and received serious head injuries and died three days later in hospital. We were all devastated and only had thoughts for his young family.

Ivor's was a career, albeit so short, that I and the thousands of fellow Cradley supporters had followed with great interest for we knew how talented he was and getting better each match. It was only the young Welshman from Berriew, Montgomeryshire's second season. The previous season had seen him start as a junior at the club. But in his second full season, he made great strides and had great confidence in his ability. He was sure he was going to be the equal of other riders in the team that year, and he proved it by his vastly improving performances on the track week in, week out. He was definitely a star in the making. Midlands' speedway writer Tom Johnson, who knew the sport inside out, was euphoric in his programme notes at Cradley and in his write-ups for the *Express and Star* of young Ivor.

Many years later, after I mentioned Ivor's name in a memorial piece in *Motor Cycle News*, I had a phone call from a member of Ivor's family, his brother I think, who thanked me so much for remembering Ivor's name in the roll call of riders who paid the ultimate price performing for us in our great sport. I am pleased to remember Ivor Hughes' name with pride in my book, for he too was a rider who touched my life. I can still see him proudly racing in his CH race jacket, and I will never forget his name.

Chapter 7

Four meetings in four days, one in Poland!

In 1970 my speedway friend Margaret, a fellow badminton player, and I had our first taste of speedway behind the Iron Curtain when the World Speedway Final was held in Wroclaw, Poland for the first time. We had a busy few days! We saw four meetings in four days! We travelled to see Cradley at Wolverhampton on Friday in the second leg of the Dudley-Wolves Trophy (which the Heathens lost 40–38 so Wolves won the trophy!) On to Swindon on Saturday night, where the Heathens, in one of their finest away performances, beat the Robins 45–33. Swede Jan Simensen on his first visit to the track, scored 13 points. Bernie Persson got a paid maximum and Roy Trigg scored 13 points. Robins' fans would say they lost because Barry Briggs was not riding, but I reckon the Heathens would still have won! After the match there followed a drive down to Gatwick for us in Margaret's old Volkswagen Beetle to catch a speedway charter plane to Poland.

In Poland, the ancient coach broke down, all the speedway fans had to get out and got it push-started. A Polish lunatic on a motorcycle hit the front of our coach, did not crash, but went down the road wringing his hand as a result of the coming together!

That journey was 105 miles and took four hours! We got stopped by the police because the driver passed a tram on the wrong side. When we eventually arrived at the grand Olympic Stadium, Wroclaw, the meeting had started, and the gates were locked. Much shouting and showing of tickets got us in and we saw Ivan Mauger win the meeting and complete his famous triple-World Championship wins in 1968, 1969 and 1970. Unique.

It was only the majestic Mauger who stopped mighty Poland on home ground from getting top spot on the rostrum with Pawel Waloszek second, just one point behind Mauger and fellow countryman Antoni Woryna third, with 50,000 Polish speed fans roaring them on. And much kidology and sportsmanship in the pits to try and put Mauger off his stride. Didn't work. Mauger was not one for turning!

Speedway was called the "black sport" in Poland, and after the meeting, we saw why. Our faces were black from the black shale that had come over the fence, and a white handkerchief became instantly black trying to wipe it off! Those were different days. No health and safety in those days. No dirt deflectors either to stop the shale from coming over the fence. But the Poles put on a magnificent spectacle with hundreds of people on the centre green dressed in gay national dress. At one stage during that trip, I was on a

Polish bus, I can't remember why, and was causing much merriment among the Polish women on the bus for some reason. I was told I was sitting on a seat reserved for pregnant women. We had another speedway meeting to complete our four in four days marathon, including the Polish World Final, and that was back at Cradley.

The club had an individual meeting on Monday night for the Watney Mann trophy. It was the first track that Mauger, who was among the field, rode as world champ, 24 hours after we'd seen him win it in Poland. Because Mauger had to attend the official banquet after the Final, he did not arrive at Heathrow till 6pm, and although he was driven straight to the track, he missed his first ride. He was very tired, but put a show on for the Midland fans, including winning one race. I believe he walked the track parading the trophy. One more memory: Margaret was a teacher and to go to Poland had taken a "sickie" from school, but her headmaster smelt a rat and spent the day making inquiries and quizzing her friends and fellow teachers, but I believe she got away with it on her special day off from the Wollaston Junior School to visit Poland for a speedway meeting.

This was the high life for me. I lived at home and was amazingly well looked after by my parents. I had a job I loved. I played badminton with a passion and became captain of the Worcestershire County third team and the Stourbridge Institute club, winning many trophies. I was following a sport I really loved and for seven years it was just sublime.

I still have a few trophies from my playing days, including the Worcestershire Badminton Association's junior tournament boys' doubles victory cup from 1963, won with my friend Martin Hill. Many trophies were won in the Cradley Heath and District badminton league, in church halls quite close to the Cradley track, one at Grainger's Lane.

Me as a callow youth, top right, in the Stourbridge Institute badminton team. Top second left Sonnu Desai, former singles champion of Bombay, who was a plastic surgeon.

It really was a doddle of a job for me at the *County Express*. I would sometimes get in by about 10am after a 10-minute ride or drive to do what Phil asked me to do:

court reporting, golden wedding or two, the occasional tragic house fire, going to the local pub to get the lowdown on council matters from the local mayor, plying him with a pint of his favourite tipple, Black Country "mixed" – half bitter, half mild ale in a pint glass. I was home for lunch most days, back to see the first edition of the evening *Express and Star* to see if we had been "scooped". A phone call, a quick re-write if we had been scooped, followed by putting the copy in a brown envelope and rushing it to the bus stop, yes, the bus, courtesy of the Midland Red bus company, where I handed the package to the conductor to be taken to Stourbridge, several miles off for collection by our head office staff from the bus garage.

That was how it was done in those days, no computers, no mobiles, no emails. You put the typewriter-written newspaper copy in a parcel on the bus! Having covered our backs, knowing we had missed no major story in our area that day, I was quite often in the snooker hall by about 3pm for a couple of hours with my reporter friend Steve, (we got quite good after so much practice), or for ten pin bowling, puffing away at "posh" Peter Stuyvesant cigarettes, home for Mum's tea and out again to play in a badminton match.

I have one particular article from the *County Express* days – which touches on my sense of humour and why I have always loved newspapers – of which I still have a cutting, and I don't suppose the now freesheet *County Express* has any problems with me quoting it here.

They've got a namecheck anyway. The cutting from 9 February 1973 reads:

"Painting – but is it art? Alderman Tom Wells (our man in the pub council "mole") asked at Dudley Council about the purchase of a painting for £185 which someone who had seen a print of it said reminded him of 'going into a public lavatory.' (For some reason).

Tom said two members of the committee who had seen a print of 'Colour Structure 71' by David Leverett had no idea what it was all about. It consisted of 'just blobs of paint.' He asked the chairman of the libraries, museums and arts committee, Cllr Dr K D Rogers if she was satisfied with the painting.

Dr Rogers said Ald Wells had taken over the mantle of Mr Ross McWhirter, the TV personality of Guinness World Records fame. She said she did not set herself up as an art critic and she added that she was not really conversant with the insides of public lavatories, either.

Dr Rogers said she would let Mr Wells know after she had seen the inside of public lavatories in the area, if there was a resemblance."

Wonderful, my sense of fun and humour and of the British provincial press at its best!

I could have done this for the rest of my days, but I didn't. I saw an advert for a speedway reporter for

Motor Cycle News in 1973, which changed my life. I had been a fervent reader of all the motorcycle newspapers and magazines which gave me a good grounding in many of the forms of motorcycle racing which are held up and down the country week in, week out at which I was a regular attender, not only of speedway, but taking in grass track racing, road racing at Mallory Park and beyond, and in particular AMCA scrambling, which was big in the Midlands, run by that doyen Don Green, who became a much loved, if acerbic, acquaintance later on.

Chapter 8

Second phase, *MCN*

I was given an interview by *Motor Cycle News* editor Peter Strong one Saturday morning in Kettering, Northants, while my friends Brian and Robert had lunch in town and we three trundled down to London afterwards for the European speedway championship at Wembley.

I was probably very lucky, as "Strongy" edited speedway for the newspaper. I got the job. It was a big decision for me; what to do. I was happy where I was, living in my hometown, at my parents' "hotel". But I accepted the huge challenge put before me and moved on to my life's Second Phase.

Peter Strong offering me my dream job on *MCN*
in a personal letter 1973

Reporter moves

A MEMBER of the County Express editorial staff at Brierley Hill and speedway reporter Mr Andrew Edwards has joined the editorial staff of Motor Cycle News, Kettering. He is an old boy of King Edward VI School Stourbridge. For 11 years he has been a member of Stourbridge Institute Badminton Club and also the Worcester League Captain. Last year he was Worcestershire County Badminton third team captain. For the coming season he was chosen for Worcestershire County as a selector but resigned because of his move He is the younger son of Mr and Mrs S. R. Edwards, of Vicarage Road, Amblecote.

County Express editorial mention of my leaving

What a culture shock, what an amazing rollercoaster ride that became in an *MCN* career which lasted for 24 years and had me – all expenses paid – visiting every country that ran speedway, reporting on most major World Championship Finals, World Pairs Finals, World Team Cup, World Long Track and Ice Speedway Championships. But once again, I was at the bottom in a newspaper office. The office junior with everything to learn, but this time in the big league, with *MCN*, EMAP's national flagship title of a huge group of car, motorcycle, gardening, fishing, country walking and other leisure titles. It was major league stuff with heady circulations and an even headier learning curve for me.

I made several trips to Kettering in Northamptonshire, where *MCN* was based, just to pick up the local *Evening Telegraph* newspaper to read the accommodation ads. There was no quick fix of looking up the paper on the internet, it hadn't been invented yet. I saw one ad offering a bedsit which seemed OK.

It turned out to be on offer from the Rev Brian Matthews in the rectory in the village of Rushton, not far from Kettering. Not really what I was anticipating or looking for, but I gave it a go and was very happy there. I never needed an alarm clock as my room was next to the kitchen and every morning the Reverend gentleman got up at around 6.30am and put on Radio Four for the news, very loudly, as he was pretty deaf.

Answering that ad did not become a quick fix; I got into village life, thinking at first that the locals were a bit "slow" after the sharp, sarcastic wit of the Black Country boys, but adjusted to the relaxed way of life in the country. I hired an old van from the Cradley area called "Rentawreck", it's true, and I took some basic furniture from Stourbridge to Rushton and Dad sat on an armchair all the way up the M6 in the front as there was no passenger seat or seatbelt! What health and safety?

I stayed in Rushton village for many more years. First with the Reverend, later sharing a rented house with John, an ex-army lawyer working as a solicitor in Kettering. Later, a second stay with the vicar after John left and even later, buying my own house in the village. John and I parted company but many years later, walking down Fleet Street, London, on what was then a very occasional visit to the capital, I bumped into John and had a chat. What an amazing coincidence that was.

Much later, I met Joy, the love of my life, who lived in Rushton with her two lovely children Cass and Vicki, and that changed my life for the better too.

We had known one another in the late 80s when she helped out behind the bar at the local pub in the village, the Thornhill Arms, and were friends from 1994, moving in together in Rushton in 1996.

We no longer live in Rushton, and there have been changes in our lives, but we are still together over 20 years later, still enjoying all the holidays we can together, including lovely times in Alderney, in the Channel Islands, and Ireland, both north and south, which we love. Daughter Vicki lived in Northern Ireland for a while, and the visits we made then were very memorable.

I even ventured over the rickety rope bridge at Carrick-a-Rede over 80 feet above the beach to Sheep's island on the Antrim coast, but at the last minute, Joy decided it was not too her, the descent onto the bridge putting her off.

We were so lucky to have a never-to-be-forgotten trip to Australia and specially Tasmania, courtesy of my lovely dad, who paid for the trip of a lifetime for Joy and I to see my brother Dave and his wife Christine and their son Mark. They made us so welcome, showed us round and we had our own hire care for a wonderful week touring the island on our own. Idyllic. What a country, what lovely people. So much beautiful scenery, the brilliant climate.

From left, me, Joy, my nephew Mark, his parents
Christine and Dave, my brother. In an Irish pub,
Launceston, their hometown then.

Joy and I on our never-to-be-forgotten trip of a
lifetime to Tasmania. This is Brady's Lookout
overlooking the River Tamar.

We loved our times too in our holiday cottage in
Norfolk, a great county of wide-open spaces, walking
as far as we could along the beaches in the summer.
Idyllic. Bacton, one of the country's great wonderful
beaches. Never crowded, even in August. Nothing lasts
forever and that cottage was sold. It gave us great
memories and a new learning curve for me as we
rented it out for holidaymakers and that caused a few
heartaches and laughs and taught me how to run a
small business.

We also holidayed in the Algarve, southern Portugal
and love that country too. Especially when daughter
Cassie lived there too. My life would have been much
sadder, much less fun, indeed unfulfilled, without Joy

and the girls, and we still help and support each other over life's sometimes rocky ground, but we have been very, very lucky. Thank you, Joy, Vicki and Cassie.

Joy and I in the garden of Midland Cottages, Rushton village, with daughters Cassie (back left) and Vicki (back right). Photo by John Hipkiss.

Chapter 9

Early *MCN* days

At *MCN*, weekends were spent reporting on meetings up and down the country, being told by my larger-than-life sports editor Scot Norrie Whyte of my assignments. As well as speedway, it could be a trial for me one week (taking my own black-and-white photos too), the odd scramble (I mean motocross!) here and there and the even more occasional road race. I see from my contract of employment, which started on 3 September 1973, my job title was "journalist – sports reporter/letters editor", nothing officially about speedway. After each event, it was back to the office to write up the copy on old ink ribbon typewriters, get the black-and-white photos printed and selected yourself before bed, quite late on many occasions. Back to the office on Monday morning for press day, to put the paper to "bed", that is to see it finished and signed off for the hungry printing presses waiting.

Not always a glamorous job. Mud - spattered jeans and shoes in the pits during another wet meeting in Vojens, Denmark, I suspect.

For many years, hot lunches with little metal lids on the plates to keep them warmish were brought to our desks from the local paper, the *Kettering Evening Telegraph* canteen, but because they reminded most of us of school dinners, we were in later years allowed a half-hour break and went to the local fish and chip restaurant en bloc! Much better. Not healthy, but good.

Tuesday was office planning day when you were told what your duties were to be that week, in a planning meeting which often meant going to see a sporting personality in the news, plus regular weekly chores like being the letters editor for me.

I'll come clean, if the post did not bring in readers' letters of good quality, my "made up" letters always got the punters back on track to disagree with often inflammatory views I'd written to get more feedback from my readers! Oops, my secret is out.

I cannot remember which speedway meeting I first covered for *MCN*, but I joined the office for the first time on the Monday morning that Peter Strong arrived back from Poland, having suffered a smashed windscreen, I seem to remember, to report on the World Speedway Final in 1973, where for once, Ivan Mauger came out second best after falling in a run-off with Poland's Jerzy Szczakiel in Katowice, Poland. One title that did get away from the great man.

Next year it was my turn to do the reporting, and I was despatched by plane to cover my first World Speedway Final in Sweden in 1974 for *MCN*. It was a pretty nervous time for me. Travelling by air for business to a foreign country to report on my first international meeting. That was Anders Michanek's year with the mighty Swede sweeping to a 15-point maximum in the Ullevi Stadium, Gothenburg. In a crowded press room, I pushed a tiny tape recorder halfway up Michanek's nose and asked if he'd had much extra practice on the track beforehand, to which he replied no, when we knew full well the Swedes had given their riders as much track time as they wanted to help their chances!

It was a dynamic performance from "Mich", who broke the track record three times during the Final. It was an awe-inspiring performance from the Swedish international, watched by a crowd of over 38,000. Nobody got anywhere near him in a faultless performance of pure speedway heaven for him and a well-earned record in the history books of championship fame. The meeting was unique in that after rain had made the track very wet, a jet-propelled car slowly lapped the circuit, drying out the red shale with its after burner! Also, a helicopter came in and helped dry the track with its rotor blades! Not quite like Cradley then!

The English riders, who I was hoping would be among the winners, were not really in the hunt, although John Louis was fourth on nine points, taking two wins, while Peter Collins was sixth, also on nine points, but without one win. Terry Betts won one race, his last, to notch six points, Dave Jessup gained five points without winning a heat. Ivan Mauger won a run-off for runner-up against Sweden's Soren Sjosten after both scored 11 points, four less than Michanek. Ole Olsen's title challenge, after a second place in his first ride, was over as early as heat five when he crashed and sustained a leg injury which forced his retirement.

One of Mauger's bikes was measured after the meeting and its capacity was found to be 0.5cc over the 500 limit, but FIM officials decided to take no action against the New Zealander, realising it was an error and wasn't performance-enhancing.

I suppose as it was the first World Speedway Final I covered for *MCN*, I always enjoyed going back to Gothenburg and loved the futuristic-looking stadium in such a wonderful, vibrant city, and despite not sometimes having the best track, it instantly brings back some of my happiest memories of travelling in Scandinavia, which I grew to love for its wonderful spaciousness, less populated, clean, no-litter streets and friendliness of its people.

As a speedway press man, I received a British Speedway Promoters' Association press pass each season, which admitted me to any track in the country. I collected bits of news snippets up and down the country on a regular basis. A typical week would see me drive to the West Midlands from the East Midlands to stay with my parents and take in a match at Cradley Heath on Saturday. Usually, an event to cover for *MCN* on a Sunday. On a Tuesday, it was a visit to dear old never-to-be-forgotten Blackbird Road, Leicester, which was a brilliant racetrack, and on to Peterborough for their home match later in the week for more high-speed speedway action. Boy, did I see lot of speedway, met loads of interesting, wonderful people. Week in, week out, each month, for years.

I covered all the major speedway events for *MCN* from World Final, semi-finals, finals, British finals, Intercontinental finals, overseas finals, Nordic-British finals, Commonwealth, British League Riders' Championship – which was often better than even the World Final – with its 16 British club number ones battling for a very prestige title at the fabulous Hyde Road track in Manchester. The old wooden stands were always filled to capacity and the mighty, excited noise of the spectators echoing together with the noise of the bikes was awe-inspiring. That memory has never left me.

The noise and the exhilaration of the special atmosphere at Belle Vue was only ever beaten by that of a Wembley World Final. Filled to capacity with 85,000 plus fans. Just walking up the tunnel in the pits, past the football dressing rooms for the first time before the Final definitely was awesome for me! I never forgot how marvellous it was either, as not so many people get the chances I had to watch history being made in the sport I loved. I had the chance to try to get the flavour of these big events in print as successfully as I could for *MCN* readers, week in and week out.

Switching forward many years, the hairs on the back of the neck feeling came upon me again as I entered the Cardiff Millennium (now Principality) Stadium just before the start of the first staging of the new World Championship GPs in 1995.

The stadium had pumping rock music, big screens, air horns (although too noisy for me and Joy, I have to say), waving flags, the excitement was all there, in an ultra-smart modern stadium, with a movable roof on, so no rain-offs. An atmosphere truly inspirational for speedway which made the eyes slightly moisten. With

Wembley gone, demolished, Cardiff ticked all the boxes for more glorious World Championship action for the modern spectators. A new great era that I saw towards the end of my journalistic career, with brilliant action, brilliant riders as ever and fantastic maxed-out TV coverage.

Pity the Cardiff hotels are so shockingly overpriced! But Saturday night in Cardiff is a jaw-dropping experience.

But back to Wembley. My first Wembley World Final was in 1975 when Ole Olsen swept to victory, with, like Michankek, a 15-point maximum.

There was a bomb scare, which turned out to be a hoax, during the meeting, but even worse was fans trying illegally to help water the track because of terribly dusty conditions. But it backfired for Britain, as well-fancied Peter Collins, after the over-exuberant track watering, in race nine, was filled in with wet shale and finished last, dashing his title hopes after two fine wins. Collins came back to win another race later, to finish fifth on 10 points, furious at how heavy watering had finished his World Final chance for another year. John Louis was an excellent third, after defeating Ivan Mauger in a run-off after both finished on 12 points, jetting from the tapes like a hero and winning in the fastest time of the night. Fellow Brit Malcolm Simmons was on 10 points, Ray Wilson on five. It was a World Championship that I think PC (Collins) could well have won but which was taken out of his grasp by those "fans" overwatering the track, a preposterous nightmare which should never have happened. There was to be another even harder to take final in 1977 when PC lost a world individual championship he should have won.

For an international meeting, the British press corps was impressive in those days. A typical turnout for a big foreign championship meeting would see staff journalists from the *Daily Express, Sunday Express*, the *Daily Telegraph, Daily Mail, Sun, Star, Daily Mirror, Sunday Mirror*, Manchester journos, plus *Motor Cycle, Motor Cycle News, Speedway Star* and a load more provincial papers' representatives following the fortunes of their own clubs' riders at home and abroad. These days, it is simply the *Speedway Star* and of course Eurosport, Sky TV and BT Sport, who have all done a brilliant job in taking speedway into the homes of millions of sports fans worldwide. The TV channels are a vital cog and a lifeline in helping to keep the name of speedway alive and in front of so many people. Speedway is heaven-sent for TV, I believe. All the action, fairly simple to televise, all in one stadium, nothing to miss. Long may it all continue. I used to make the office staff laugh when I'd say if a speedway race was boring, another one would be starting soon, which would be a cracker. But if you had a dull Grand Prix road race it was dull for hours.

That was the sort of press turn out for 1976 when we all went behind the Iron Curtain to Katowice, Poland, not knowing what a sensational event it would turn out to be for Britain, British speedway, and Peter Collins in particular.

I'd got to know PC pretty well and was ghosting his column in *MCN*. He was so easy-going that it was difficult to get him to say anything in his column in those days, let alone say something controversial!

My friendship with Peter let me place an *MCN* sticker on the left side of his fuel tank for that mega final, so the name of *Motor Cycle News* was carried on the bike that took him to victory in front of the biggest crowd ever seen for a World Speedway Final, for nothing, which was put at a staggering 100,000 to 120,000. Now with all the mega-sponsorship that would never happen today, would it? I believe it was by far the biggest crowd that has ever watched a speedway world Final and to look out over the top of the open terraces was an incredible sight. I mean, they only get around 120,000 people watching a MotoGP at the big races and they are spread round an over two-mile tarmac track.

Peter Collins, world champion 1976, Katowice, Poland with
the *MCN* sticker I gave to PC proudly on his fuel tank.
Behind is Belle Vue boss Jack Fearnley.

Collins started with a win in heat three in a new
track record while passing Doug Wyer and Jiri Stancl
in one manoeuvre on the second circuit. He broke the
track record again in his second race, heat seven,
despite having to pass under John Louis on the first
corner of lap two and under Malcolm Simmons on the
last lap. The Belle Vue rider in race nine took a win
from the tapes for a change and victory was on for him.
It was a wait until heat 14 for PC and he again took
victory from Scott Autrey, Phil Crump and Valeri
Gordeev. Four unbeaten rides for 12 points. The world
title was just over 70 seconds away for Collins.

The climax for Collins came fittingly in the last race of the night, race 20. In the most important race of his young life, Collins entered the realm of the shale greats by taking a tactical second place to give him the mega title by one point, after Ivan Mauger made a great gate to take an early lead. But PC wisely settled for second place which gave him his great win.

After Peter's win, the first British win since the late Peter Craven's 14 years ago in 1962, it was difficult but essential to remain professional and not jump up and down too much. We all had our jobs to do after the meeting, interviewing our new world champion and the other Brits, including the late Malcolm Simmons, another Brit, who finished second to Peter that day, John Louis who scored nine points, Doug Wyer on eight and Chris Morton with six. That's right, five of the 16 riders in a World Final field were Brits. Now those really were heady days for us British pressmen. That's why I call it my golden era.

I bet Mort never again ate a Polish hot dog, for the one he ate during practice had more gristle and fat in it than "meat". If he had done, he mightn't have been around to mastermind the emergence of Belle Vue in their new National Speedway Stadium!

My breakfast was just as bad in Poland. Simmons and his wife and I waited for ages for our boiled eggs in a Polish hotel but when they were served up, they were virtually raw and cold and were uneatable! And Simmo had a World Final to ride in later.

Earlier, years ago, one famous British speedway journalist on his visits to Poland would just take sandwiches with him from home which he lived on for the entire trip. He would eat nothing local from Poland at all. Poland could not at that time cater for the tastes of Western delicate stomachs, unlike today's cosmopolitan country.

MCN used the world's best speedway photographer, Mike Patrick from the *Speedway Star*, for its pictures and I tried to help after the 76 Final by humping the famous Winged Wheel trophy, then presented to each winner, around the hotel that evening for Mike to get his brilliant photos of Peter with the iconic mounted speedway wheel, lined up together with wife-to-be, Angela. It was unfair, I think, that speedway's world trophy was later on gifted to Ivan Mauger for his World Championship winning exploits. I reckon the authorities should have given the great Ivan a lovely replica and kept presenting the Winged Wheel trophy to each year's world champion. It was the best speedway trophy of that generation, so lovely in its almost modern art deco simplicity.

Peter's win was life-changing for him, and he went on to become one of the greatest riders of all time, and his abilities on a bike are legendary. From his early days as a leading grass track rider, right through to the World Final win, his world team championship contributions for England, and world pairs. I feel privileged to have seen him ride many times in all disciplines and achieve greatness. He took in his stride a ride on the infamous two-stroke Yamaha TZ750 American flat tracker at the 1980 British grass track GP at Hereford, which was so fast and dangerously difficult to ride that its normal pilot, the legendary Kenny Roberts, once said Yamaha couldn't give him enough money for him to ride it! Luckily for Roberts, the two-stroke was banned by the American authorities at the end of 1975 after just one year in competition, when the class became for two-cylinder bikes only (the TZ had a four-cylinder 130bhp road race engine in its spindly frame). Peter rode it as part of a team of dirt track Yamahas which took on a squad of Triumph 750s. Peter got third and a fourth places and never got it out of second gear; what power, he said! The most fierce bike I ever saw raced.

I met the great Kenny Roberts when he visited our offices in Kettering, and we took him to the pub. He was great company, very sharp, quick-witted, polite, a lovely man. He just did seem different, he had an aura about him, not arrogance, but just being in his presence you felt honoured to be with a great man and share his time. One of the greatest road racers of all time and I'm glad I can say I met him once or twice. And, of course, he was one of the great US dirt track riders of all time as well. I'm afraid we got him a little tiddly on strong British beer, which I'm sure he was totally unused to. I remember him saying, "Another beer, barkeep!"

Peter Collins was pretty laid back when not racing, but his sharp mind and impish sense of humour never changed throughout his life. I still have and cherish a

Polish hotel napkin, now brown with age, signed by Peter the night before he won the 1976 World Final. It says: "To Andrew, best wishes Peter Collins." Then he added, "Pphhh?" not taking the task at all seriously! The napkin is slipped into a photo of Peter and I at his bike shop opening.

All his brothers were to some extent laid back too, and I got to know them all. What with Phil riding for "my" club Cradley Heath, then there were Les and Neil, and I had a soft spot for the baby of the family, young Stephen, who also rode for the Heathens and was just as amiable (perhaps even more so) as the rest of the family. I enjoyed our little chats in the pits at Cradley during Stephen's time there. Maybe too nice, not enough "edge" to make it on track, but he gave it his very best shot and was a delightful, polite young man, having come successfully through the junior grass tracking ranks. It was a different era then when Stephen tried to make it, of course. As brother Peter said, when he started, he could buy a £350 bike off Briggo (Barry Briggs) and could ride with the best, but progress happened and with it came the expenses of Stephen's era, where the sport's engine tuners earned big money from anyone wanting to enter the sport successfully, even from the juniors wanting to break into the sport. It became a tough, expensive call, did speedway racing.

Stourbridge, near Cradley, became Stephen's home, and during Covid, he was on the frontline working in an NHS hospital. Bless you, Stephen.

But it's onto the next stage of Peter's story. On a wet and wild night in the futuristic Ullevi Stadium, Gothenburg, Sweden, Peter rode out of his skin to finish second in the World Final, defending his title on 13 points. But the story behind the headline is remarkable. For Peter had broken his left leg in a second-half race only days before on a loose iron drainage cover (over two feet wide, a foot wide and an inch thick) which had become dislodged by watering and crept over the inside edge of the Belle Vue track. 200 stitches were needed inside his leg and 32 outside stitches were needed in the wound after he hit it in the awful accident. The leg had been sliced to the bone and included a compound fracture of the fibula. How could anyone walk let alone ride a World Final with an injury like that? Peter did.

In Sweden, for once, Peter made super starts. He'd won his opening two rides and was leading Ole Olsen in his third, but the Dane swooped down on Peter on the inside, and the brave Englishman knew he had to get his injured leg out of the way and Olsen was through. Peter ran second to Ivan Mauger in his next race but another win, his third of the evening, in terrible wet, slimy conditions gave him second overall while Mauger won the meeting to claim his fifth crown, equalling the feat of Ove Fundin. The superb effort of Peter that night was one of the championship's grittiest performances I ever witnessed, as he hobbled round the pits on crutches, in so much pain, between his races. He was on top form and, but for that terrible handicap, I am sure he would have claimed a second title. Another title that was taken away from PC, in my opinion, was in 1975. He was so close to becoming a three-time world champion. But as PC later admitted, he was crazy to ride in a Final with a broken leg.

Peter had the most glittering career of all of the British riders I got to know through *MCN*, and his record shows he won 10 world championships. I am proud to say I was present at most of his glorious wins. Proud for him and for what he did for British speedway at a time when Britain was definitely the most successful speedway country. He had started as a kid in grass track racing as they all did in those days and won his first trophy for finishing second in the 250 class in the North West Centre championship and went onto win British grass track championships.

Peter Collins at speed, Hereford grass track 1977.
Taken by me.

In addition to his individual world title, Peter won four World Championship pairs titles for England in 1977 (with Malcolm Simmons), 1980 (Dave Jessup), 1983 (Kenny Carter), 1984 (Chris Morton), alongside his remarkable record in the World Team Cup which he helped England win in 1973, 1974, 1975, 1977 and 1980. In 1973, 1974 and 1975, he recorded three consecutive maximums (unbeaten by any rider). What a great achievement by the world's leading rider. Domination of world team speedway on a grand scale.

He also claimed the British championship in 1979. He says of that night: "This was the one that nearly eluded me! The British title was something I had tried to win for so many times that it was a great feeling when I made it. It gave me a great sense of achievement to get the lot. It took me the longest – nine years." He has also won the British League Riders' Championship, 1974 and 1975, and in 1974 was European champion followed by Intercontinental titles in 1976 and 1977. The following year, in 1979, he was also crowned World Masters Champion. While domestically, Peter took the Northern Riders championship three times in 1974, 1975 and 1977, with wins in the prestige Internationale at Wimbledon in 1974 and 1978, followed by wins in the Pride of the East title at King's Lynn and the Wolverhampton staged Olympique, both in 1976, his World Championship winning year. For his club Belle Vue, he really was the Ace helping them to win British League titles in 1971, 1972 and 1982.

He only once claimed the British championship but took British League Riders' Championship gold medals on his home track of Hyde Road, Belle Vue, 1974 and 1975 in meetings which everyone knew had far higher quality fields in those days than World Finals. In 1980, banner headlines in *MCN* shouted out: "The greatest speedway rider of the decade," by Andrew Edwards, and yes, the story was all about Peter. Peter recalled the amazing incident at Wembley in the World League Final in 1973. Peter said: "Yet another memorable run-off with Anders Michanek. This time the setting was Wembley after England and Sweden had drawn 39-all in the Final of the international tournament. It was my first time at Wembley, and the time I really 'arrived' on the international scene. It was a great honour to be asked to take part in the run-off as I was the youngest there. It was pretty dramatic too, I ended up in a pile on the pits bend and was awarded the race with Mich excluded." The second run-off with Michanek that year was for the Knockout Cup Final. Peter said: "The last race to settle this cup final between Belle Vue and Reading is one that stands out in my career. Michanek and I had a match race to battle for the result, and I won on the line after he had passed each other 16 times in four laps! I rode with a broken left hand and had the clutch transferred to the throttle side." Totally amazing memories. To say that it was a heroic effort belittles the circumstances of his win that day. He thought of the idea after remembering a childhood Lambretta scooter which had the clutch and gears mounted on the right-hand throttle side.

Even a broken handlebar didn't faze Peter when in 1972 he had to ride one-handed, holding onto the front fork leg against Newport, and still won the race.

After his career, Peter did many stints with Sky in their superb coverage of the sport, giving his exclusive champion's viewpoint to the viewers. When, finally, Hyde Road bit the dust and was sold off as a car auction site, it was mainly Peter's heroic efforts, among others who were on hand to help Belle Vue to find another home, up the road at Kirkmanshulme stadium, where the Aces had originally ridden. Without that action from Peter, Belle Vue's name could have gone forever. Belle Vue should remember that. Kirky Lane served them well, was the favourite track of Ace Jason Crump for a while, until the new purpose-built National Stadium was built in Manchester, the new home of the Aces club in 2016.

In November 2001, Peter, not before time, was made an MBE for his great services to motorcycle racing. One trophy Peter won is often overlooked and that is the Segrave Trophy. It is a unique trophy, awarded annually for great achievements on land, sea or in the air.

Peter and his Weslake engine tuner Dave Nourish were the winners of the Segrave Trophy after his World Championship solo win in 1976. The legendary designer Harry Weslake, the founder of the Weslake engine dynasty, also received a special Segrave medal.

The trophy honours the great British racing driver Sir Henry Segrave and was first won in 1930. It is perhaps the most prestigious trophy that can be awarded to a sportsman and indeed the roll of honour that Peter joined in 1976 shows just that. Included for the daring exploits are motorcycle TT hero Geoff Duke (1951), Donald Campbell (1955), Sir Stirling Moss (1957), Donald Campbell (1964 and posthumously 1966), Bruce McLaren (1969), Jackie Stewart (1973), Barry Sheene, the year after Peter in 1977, then again in 1984, followed by World Championship motorcycle racer Mike Hailwood (1979), and Martin Brundle (1988). What a fantastic list Peter joined, and he became only the second bike man to win it after Geoff Duke. The late and great TT hero Joey Dunlop was given the trophy posthumously in 2000. Other biking heroes who were awarded the Segrave Trophy were John McGuinness in 2015 for his amazing Isle of Man TT record, the late John Surtees OBE in 2012 for his exploits in winning world title on two and four wheels, and Carl Fogarty MBE in 1994 for winning the World Superbike Championship with Ducati, and World Championship sidecar driver Steve Webster MBE in 1991.

Chapter 10

MCN office for japes

MCN was not a normal office. If you were into japes, you were in.

Some of the journalists were very good riders, Chris Moss the head of the road riding test fleet thought nothing of 60mph wheelies up and down the one-way street outside the office building, cheered on by the rest of the staff.

A trials bike appeared once in the reporters' room, having been ridden up the back stairs and into the building and left on top of one of the editorial desks. Good job that at the time it was quite an old, dilapidated building. A Burton shop tailor's dummy was pinched from a skip, I think I might have had something to do with that, and dressed up in complete motorcycle gear, including helmet. It was placed in the editor's chair in his office, ready to scare the life out of him when he opened his door and turned on the light on a Sunday night to be confronted by this figure behind his desk! It worked too; he jumped a mile.

Many years later, I met fellow *MCN* reporter Chris Dabbs, and he informed me that he thought my philosophy during my time there was to keep "just under the radar", a reference to maybe not always going along with the crowd, but not something I'd consciously done! Chris also said I was quite famous for my disappearing acts, which prompted plenty of jovial comment. Someone would apparently ask, "Where's Andrew?" And the reply was, "He must be around, or he's coming back, because his coat is on the back of his chair." But apparently, I'd be at home!

I honestly don't remember any of this! But it sounds devious enough to be true.

Photographers can be a funny breed. My theory is that in the days when they did their own printing in darkrooms, they became affected by the fumes of the fixing chemicals which accounted for their funny moods. I was lucky in that the photographers who helped me in my speedway and grass track coverage were terrific people and became lifelong friends.

In the very early Cradley days, I met up with John Hipkiss, who took black-and-white mug shots of the Cradley team as a hobby for the supporters to buy. He was a lathe operator by profession, I think. I asked for some of his snaps which were published, and that was how John got started in speedway press photography. He became one of the star snappers in the country, taking shots for *MCN* in all disciplines too not just speedway, and for the *Speedway Star* for many years.

Me in my Macau jacket, this time in the Czech Republic
for the World Long Track Final.

John Hipkiss' favourite photo taken in a split second
of Rick Miller's entire engine exploding from the
frame during a race at the Tommy Knudsen farewell
Coventry speedway. Amazing shot!

Many a Sunday night would be spent in John's Birmingham house waiting for him to develop his films in his darkroom at the bottom of his garden, ready for me to jump in my car and return to Kettering to finish writing up the story. This was pre-digital photography, when action shots were an art, on 35mm black-and-white film on a 36-shot roll! That was all the chances you got. 36 pictures. We certainly had some amazing times going up and down the country together, reporting and taking pictures of not only speedway but the big grass track events, including Ian Barclay's brilliant Ace of Aces meeting and the amazing, boarded circuit at Collier Street in Kent. John became a valued friend and colleague and took the photo of Joy, Vicki, Cassie and me, which I still have today. Thanks, John, me old mate. One of the best. He went on to successfully mastermind his own freelance photography business, working all hours that God sent him, mainly in the West Midlands, before retiring to Thailand.

John Hipkiss in Prague, taking the photos for the World Long Track Championships for *MCN*.

John Hall, an Evesham postman, was another lovely character who also took photographs at Cradley as a hobby and helped me out for many years. In his lovely Worcestershire country drawl, he'd sidle up and say, "Want some grass?" No, he wasn't offering drugs, but telling us the new crop of asparagus was ready and did we want some. You bet; it was the best 'grass' in the world! He'd often pop round to my mum and dad's house and drop off some country fresh veg for them from the Vale of Evesham, including the famous asparagus. They thought the world of him. He too became a valued friend and a great asset for *MCN* for photo shoots.

There was of course *MCN*'s own photographer, John "Selwyn" Noble, who was a larger-than-life character. He was a top-class professional man who could get the best shots of just about anyone around at the time, although he liked a little moan now and again. He covered everything with his immense, long-lens cameras, from motocross, road racing, trials, even sometimes speedway and grass track. There is always one thing I can remember about John; he knew before almost anyone else what was going to happen next, who the next editor was, the latest gossip, anything to do with *MCN*, and 99 per cent of the time he was right. He definitely had his ear to the ground at all times did our Selwyn. And a legendary eater. He once had a gigantic steak and chips, then called over the waiter and said, "Same again please!" and ate a second dinner. In his youth, he was a great sea swimmer. He told me he used to swim down the coast from his home in

Happisburgh, Norfolk, to Bacton, where I once had my holiday rental home. Great sea swimming.

During my time at *MCN*, Cecil Bailey was a top photographer the office used, mostly for southern events and not all speedway. I remember when I met him, he had a very high-pitched voice. I was told when he was a child, he'd had an accident to his ear, not that it affected his voice of course, and a doctor performed surgery on his head on the kitchen table.

But the revelation was he'd been a pioneer speedway rider too. He rode for Southampton in 1948–49 and Plymouth and Southampton in 1950. Cecil was also an expert trials and grass track rider. He died in 2008.

Many years after his retirement, he was at a speedway track and despite just having a suit on was persuaded to have a go round the track on a bike. To the astonishment of all concerned, this little "old boy" had not lost it, and jaws dropped open as he broadsided round at enthusiastic speed! Amazing.

Speedway Star chief photographer Mike Patrick also became a firm friend of mine during most of the years I spent reporting on continental events.

We always seemed to room together in our foreign jaunts which worked well for both of us, I think. At one stage, Mike wanted to do long-distance running and always packed his shorts and running shoes.

Mike was already a thin beanpole of a bloke and he got on well with his training, getting up early before we had to start work to pound kilometres of foreign pavements. Unfortunately, he began to lose weight through so much training and couldn't put the weight back on despite eating well, and he had to give up his marathon running.

I always teamed up with the *Speedway Star* team when they went to world events. Phil Rising, Richard Clark and Mike put up with me tagging along for years, getting me air tickets and travelling with the ace Star team, for which I am eternally grateful.

You couldn't keep us off the golf course in our travels, mini golf that is. Richard Clark, *Speedway Star*, left, Mike Patrick, *Star* photographer, centre, and Bert Harkins, former rider, right. This course was near Vetlanda, Sweden.

Some of the jaunts were memorable. Some distinctly uncomfortable. I think it was Phil who had a "good idea" for the entire British press corps to travel to Wroclaw, Poland, by coach in 1992. About 20 press men went on the madcap tour through Europe, travelling for days to get to Poland and the World Final. That was okay, but then we had to do all those hard, gruelling, hundreds and hundreds of miles back again.

At least we could write up our stories in the bus, me hammering away on my trusty portable typewriter, which passed plenty of time. For some reason, Peter Collins came back with us on the coach, and I remember looking down at an ungodly hour of the night to find him asleep under my legs!

When the chemical toilet got full, it needed to be emptied but we did not have time to stop because of our tight deadline, so the contents were tipped out of the coach door on the move by the driver's mate, I guess! That's what I remember anyway.

World final venues came in all shapes and sizes over the years. Some were terrific places like Munich (1989) in the sumptuous Olympic football stadium, although the temporary laid track was not to everyone's taste. Los Angeles Coliseum (1982), the first time the Final had been granted to America was fabulous, even if only 30,000 attended. American showbiz glitz at its best with a "spaceman" with a rocket backpack shooting up in the air, followed by stagecoaches on the pre-meeting parade. Promoter Ivan Mauger, Barry Briggs and Harry Oxley, the Costa Mesa promoter, pulled out all the stops for a great event and were rewarded with the most debated race ever seen in the entire history of the championship.

Bradford's giant Odsal Stadium put on a very good display in 1985, but Britain did produce the worst ever World Final poster. Then there were others which were not up to the mark as international venues for speedway's greatest one-off finals. Places like the country track Norden in Germany, 1983. Literally middle of nowhere surrounded by fields. Amsterdam's crumbling, old Olympic stadium, which was way past its best when speedway held its only two-day Final in 1987 is another of speedway's "misses" along with another German track way out in the sticks at Pocking, 1993. But all events provided memorable world champions, cheered on by thousands of speedway devotees.

At a German event, we were very late leaving the track and got lost several times trying to find our little hotel. About 1 am we went past a roadside red-light district, only to get lost and somehow go past the girls again! We found the little hotel right out in the sticks and it was shut tight, not a light on anywhere. Much banging on doors and windows brought a light in an upstairs window with a teenage girl moodily calling down to us. Luckily one of our party, Keir Radnedge of the *Daily Mail*, spoke German and got her to open the front door and room keys were grabbed off their hooks for some much-needed sleep.

On one visit to Lonigo, Italy, the hire car driven by Mike Patrick, with me and former Scottish rider Bert Harkins, broke down on the autostrada. Unfortunately, it was over 90 degrees in the middle of the day, no shade, no hats, no water. It took hours for Mike to get it sorted and another car was hired. As Bert said, "We all nearly died that day!" *Star* editor Phil Rising went out looking for us as he was concerned at our non-appearance and he had an accident with a scooter.

We missed practice as well.

In the Italian sunshine before a Lonigo meeting, back left: Bert Harkins, back right: Phil Rising, *Speedway Star* managing editor. Front left: British speedway promoter Terry Russell, Bert's wife Edith, and Richard Clark, *Star* editor.

At Munich in 1989, for some reason no member of the British press was allowed press passes to get in to report on their meeting. We should have known it was going to be tough when we met England team managers Eric Boocock and Colin Pratt walking towards us, away from the stadium, swearing and cussing, saying they hadn't been able to get in and were going back to the hotel. "Stuff them," they said as they huffed off. It was no better for us. Voices were raised, much shouting occurred. Accusations made, fingers pointed. Despite all accreditations being correct, FIM passes produced, still nobody was getting in. The organisers just refused to let anyone in.

What seemed like hours later, we were all issued with tickets and we could get on with our jobs. And threats were made that when the German press came to Wembley for the next World Final, they wouldn't be allowed in either! It all got very silly and unnecessary, all we wanted was to do the jobs we'd all been sent to do.

I remember being upset just after the press conference. Some members of the hangers-on "press" from the UK, which speedway has always had, couldn't wait to pull down the posters behind the riders for souvenirs while journalists were still working in the room, interviewing them. Disgusting. They let their country down and themselves with their bad manners and shouldn't have been in the press conference in the first place.

Mike Kilby was a great stalwart photographer for *MCN*. He was sent on assignments all over the country each weekend for many years by *MCN* bosses. He would be at some trial, scramble, grass track or speedway with me week in, week out, for many years.

Mike had a wonderful, infectious laugh and a great Wiltshire brogue. Always smoking his rollups and never without a flat cap, inside or out of the house.

More often than not, Mike was accompanied by his friend who had a Rover V8 with a 3500cc Buick engine, a very sporty and now desirable car. It ran on five-star petrol, which was at that time being phased out by the petrol companies, so if only four-star was on offer, they had to get the bonnet up and retard the ignition to make it run.

After a grass track or speedway on a Sunday, I used to drop Mike off at his Swindon home and while cups of tea were drunk, sometimes he'd go and develop his rolls of film for me, saving a job for the darkroom technician back at the office.

Mike's brother was speedway rider Bob Kilby, another extrovert. He was an excellent, fearless rider who had spells with Swindon and Exeter and for a while he was in the *Guinness Book of Records* as the world's fastest speedway rider as he was track-record holder of the fastest track in the country at the time, Exeter's County Ground.

One year at Leicester, Bob won, I think it was a British World Championship semi-final and he had a particularly fine evening, winning the meeting. Mike had travelled to the meeting with his brother. But during the meeting, Mike became very ill with asthma and his trusty 'puffer' and a couple of brandies didn't make him feel much better as he sat in Bob's van in the pits for some of the meeting. Professional to the end, he got a last photo of his brother on the podium and handed me the film before Bob, who had been alerted by me to the situation, dashed straight off, no celebrations, no explanations, and got in the car to drive his brother home as quickly as he could. They made it back to Swindon in double quick time and I know Mike was so grateful to his brother, who didn't stop to chat and bask in his wonderful success that night, but just couldn't wait to get his brother home to bed and rest and thankfully recover. It was a very lovely compassionate act by Bob that night. Top man. Always was. When Bob died at an early age, it was a tragedy for British speedway, and I loved him and his brother dearly. What a family, who helped and supported British speedway so much.

Bob also competed on the grass and he told me his secret at making great starts at a particular meeting run by a certain club. "Kilb" always used to slay the opposition there every time. The starter was a pipe smoker and just before he prepared to pull the lever to raise the tapes, he had a habit of clenching the pipe in his mouth, so when Bob, ever the slick operator, saw the pipe start to go up in the chap's mouth, he had already started to drop the clutch and was straight into the lead. Worked a treat every time, said Bob. I bet he got a lot of extra prize money by working out that little trick, shooting from that elastic starting tape like a whippet every time before everyone else in the race had moved. Smart operator was Bob. One of the great characters of speedway who I still miss.

Mike died, and at the last grass track meeting I saw him, he was not working, and I am sad to say from a distance, I didn't recognise him at first, he was so thin and gaunt. He shuffled off wearing his *MCN* black jacket. I never saw him again.

Bob, as tough as he was during his entire speedway career, suffered from ill health and died at 64. I was so pleased to see Bob's son Lee publish his own book on his father's illustrious career. A lovely treasure.

Chapter 11

MCN story

Motor Cycle News started in 1955 (as *Motorcycle News*), the brainchild of the brilliant publisher Cyril Quantrill. And I am proud to say that I was a staff man for 24 of those years.

But back to the beginnings, before I joined. *MCN*, as it became known, was a prickly young upstart back in 1955, with two already established weeklies, *The Motor Cycle* (Iliffe Press) and *Motor Cycling* (Temple Press) which came out on Thursdays and didn't do much in the way of coverage of motorcycle sport, it was for the road rider with informative road tests etc.

Quantrill, who had been employed by *Motor Cycling*, spotted a niche in the market. His magazine started with only a short run of around 3,000 copies. But it came out on a Wednesday, a day earlier than the other two weeklies, and had lots of up-to-date news and scoops based around the sport of motorcycling, as well as news for road bikers.

It was a ground-breaking formula, which proved a great success and went on to get bigger. The publisher EMAP saw great potential in this new magazine and bought it from Quantrill in 1956 (but with the great man retained as editor). When Quantrill resigned in 1961, circulation stood at 67,000. And it was to rise again and again until it reached over 100,000 copies per week. It was one of the shrewdest moves the Peterborough-based media giant ever made. From the late 60s, *MCN* masthead was blue with the famous old-fashioned goggles and helmet motif proudly displayed. A wonderful image, known throughout motorcycling. Never one to stand still, *MCN* changed dramatically to red and yellow punk colours in the 70s and had lots more colour in its vibrant pages. Its rival became *Motor Cycle Weekly* but IPC closed it in 1983. *MCN* was the master of motorcycle weekly journalism. *MCN* was EMAP's flagship for many years and was its greatest revenue maker. And to this day, *MCN* is still the ground-breaking leader of 'motorcycles for sale' ads in the country, although EMAP's consumer division became the property of Bauer Media in 2008.

After its initial life in a little office off Fleet Street, *MCN* moved to sleepy East Midlands town Kettering, an old shoe-manufacturing town, which was hated by *MCN* journo and *Classic Bike* editor Mike Nicks, who slagged it off again in 2015 in his then regular *Classic Bike* magazine column! Far removed from his beloved California where he worked in the bike scene in the sunshine for many years. But some of us stuck it out and enjoyed the rolling, understated countryside of Northamptonshire and its neighbouring county Leicestershire, although he still has a point about "Ket'rin" town.

Motor Cycle News staff "do" for reporter Peter Howdle.
Me, bottom, second right.

During the 24 years of my time with *MCN*, we had three offices in the town. The first one, where I had my interview with editor Peter Strong, was in Huxloe Place, above Burton the tailor's shop, which had been a pub (the White Swan) I believe. The iron frame for the hanging pub sign is still seen from the street on the first floor.

Our editorial office had the best sprung dance floor in the town, apparently.

The office entrance was up an alley, full of the pungent aroma you get from hot metal and ink where the offices and print works of the *Evening Telegraph*, owned by EMAP provincial newspapers, stood for many years. We worked for EMAP in the national newspaper division, so we felt "one-up" over the local journos. Prima donnas!

In those early days there was a large reporters' room, with the editor's "office" a cubicle in the corner with the secretary and her assistants in another room. In the reporters' room, there were old-fashioned wooden desks, huge clanky typewriters and many, many phones, which enabled up to keep in touch with whatever was happening in the world of motorcycle sport. Always on the lookout for that "exclusive" front-page story, written up in tabloid hype, which as I say, was a winning formula for all of *MCN*'s working life at the top of motorcycle sport journalism. Not for us the swanky Fleet Street life in London, although that of course was not to last much longer and soon became a much harder life at "Wapping" as the new era of digital publishing revolution got underway, with many changes.

We had further spells at Northfield Avenue, the brand-new home of the *Kettering Evening Telegraph* with *MCN* tagging along as well, in our own section of the building where "new technology" had to be learnt, while we still had to get the paper week in, week out. Out went the old noisy typewriters and in came computers, the start of the desktop newspaper revolution. Not quite so state-of-the-art was the fact that the mainline trains, when they thundered by at the back of the building, did make it shake quite perceptibly, I seem to remember! But the Northfield adventure was a move too far as it turned out.

We got caught up in a journalists' strike, which was a National Union of Journalists action for the cause of the provincial journalists. It had nothing to do with us, but as fellow NUJ members we were put in an impossible situation. Solidarity was okay, but we felt it was not our fight. It was a difficult time with picket lines and fellow journalists on strike, but we felt we could not support them like that and not get *MCN* out, losing the company hundreds of thousands of pounds a week.

It was not about our pay and conditions; it was their fight, we thought. The NUJ was very political in those days and had great Marxist leanings, which was sometimes very difficult for some of its members, more inclined to be more liberal.

We wanted to continue to work. But picket lines were not to be crossed by fellow union members. It was a big dilemma for many of us. At this time a few of us led by chief reporter Norrie Whyte went to put our views to the NUJ at its plush London offices, but when we were talking to the big boss of the union, Norrie unfortunately mentioned we were thinking of joining the opposition, Institute of Journalists "union", which was a terribly bad move. We were all of us dramatically shown the door by the boss of our own union! Out on our ears, back in the street. For a short while, as a stopgap measure, *MCN* was produced from a series of people's homes, including I remember Jerry Clayton's house in Kettering and Peter Strong's cottage in Brigstock. The *MCN* editorial team had a secret meeting with EMAP MD Robin Miller (now Sir Robin) himself an ex-*MCN* teenage reporter. The upshot was we said to Sir Robin if he'd give us our own office, away from the provincial journalists, we would continue working to publish *MCN* as normal. He saw the sense of it immediately, being one of the shrewdest entrepreneur businessmen I have ever met, and we quickly moved out of Northfield Avenue, away from any anguish caused by the possibility of having to cross picket lines of the provincial paper journalists. Not very ethical, but that was our practicality.

We went back to Huxloe Place after it was quickly refurbed for use by *MCN* only, before more modern offices in Station Road were bought for the paper to use. It was still in the town and very handily placed next to the rail station with its hourly service to St Pancras Station, London, and access to *MCN*'s London advertising office. The editorial office was on the first floor, and us reporters had to give a lift to wheelchair-bound staff man Chris Dabbs up the steps in his wheelchair. Don't tell Health and Safety.

I worked with many editors during my time in editorial. "Strongy" was a real grafting worker, very good at his job and ready too for a good laugh when it was appropriate. His period was a happy go lucky time, when the main influence on my work was sports reporter Norrie Whyte. It was he, in those days, who held the office together. He was a very forceful six-foot-plus roly-poly Scot, who knew everybody there was to know in motorcycle sport worldwide, especially in road racing, the Blue Riband of all racing for MCN. And he was the undisputed King of the paddocks for many years. Different minds work in different ways, but I do remember Norrie's desk was always clean, tidy with no paper on it at all; he binned everything, while my desk was inches thick in pieces of paper, press releases, collecting dust week after week. He had what you might call a gruff persona and didn't suffer fools at all. He liked to be in charge. And liked a drop of whiskey. At Christmas time in the Huxloe Place office which looked down on the town's High Street, there was a Santa Claus, not the real one, who kept playing the same carols over and over again on a tape cassette machine. Possibly having come back from a lunchtime pint, Norrie got fed up with this noise and flinging wide the first-floor window, he bellowed down to the surprised chap in a Santa suit trying to help a worthy charity, to pack up his irritating carols tape and go forth – somewhere else. And he did, to the applause and grateful thanks of the rest of the editorial staff. Norrie was after all a Scot, and Christmas was nothing but a practice for him; the proper celebration was New Year, which he took very seriously.

Not only in my view, but most other people in the profession thought Norrie was the best news and sports editor in motorcycling history, bar none. It was a tragic waste of talent when later on in his career, he was, in my view, "demoted" to cover trials and not road racing when office politics came into play. "They", the bosses, who had none of his vast knowledge and terrific newspaper know-how, learned the hard way over decades, thought he was too big for his boots, I believe. But Norrie was outwardly stoic about it all, saying it was a lot easier to report on than road racing. One call to the world champion each week, he told me, and the column was done! Same wages I bet, less work, I reckon; pretty good for a dour Scotsman, who never gave much away.

Norrie liked a drink and if he wasn't propping up the bar with people like "Yer Maun" Joey Dunlop or members of the press and motorcycle companies or riders, he could get up to mischief. It was Norrie, at the 1971 TT, who started a legendary wind-up of a young, female reporter sent to cover the Isle of Man races for the first time from the *Sunday Times*, I believe. At a bar one evening, probably the legendary Castle Mona Hotel, the party was getting pretty merry with maybe a small party of around 10 people representative of top motorcycle companies and *MCN*'s other inimitable reporting force, John Brown. But it was Norrie who started talking about a rider who he called Edgar Jessop.

Norrie told the young reporter, Jessop had won the 1927 Senior TT on a Norton, wearing plimsolls as he was too poor to buy proper racing boots. Not only that but the Norton had a supercharger off a Bentley car fitted. She wrote all this down in her notebook, egged on by everyone in the party, adding bits to the story in serious tones. Of course, it was totally fabricated, made up for the ears of the gullible reporter! Only at the end of the evening did someone tell her she'd been "had" in a big way; it was all a very big wind-up.

It has not been forgotten by some, who had ties made with initials "EJ" and a plimsoll for those who had been in on the joke. I don't suppose it interfered with the young reporter's career. Thirty-six years later my friend Paul Fowler, fellow *MCN* reporter, told me he reckoned he still had the late John Brown's Edgar Jessop tie in his possession. And in a Sydney speedway programme later on, impish Nigel Boocock on tour with the British Lions in Australia, wrote in the programme that Edgar Jessop was going to put in an appearance to help the team. Great sense of humour "Booey" had and a great wind-up merchant. Him and "EJ" would have got on well.

Paul, who was at *MCN* from 1974–85, was a sub-editor, motocross and Grand Prix road race reporter during that time and we always got on well. He had a varied life, was at one time a publican, actor, and a freelance drama adjudicator and independent funeral celebrant, and very good he is at that from personal experience from a couple of funerals I attended. From the University of Essex, he earned a BA in drama and literature (2001–2004).

Back to Norrie for another story. Editor Peter Law, I believe trying to flex his muscles as a "new man" to the job, insisted one year in arranging the travel and ticket arrangements for *MCN*'s annual trip to the mighty Assen TT in the Netherlands. Another famous *MCN* road trip each year, similar to the Isle of Man TT, although not as massive an undertaking for *MCN* as that to Mona's Isle, with our annual Marching Orders.

I think Peter must have put Norrie's back up, not a good thing to do, as it was a job he performed admirably year in year out for GP travel arrangements without error. Norrie knew that Peter had made a mistake with the 24-hour clock in getting ferry tickets but didn't let on and the party of himself, Peter and photographer John Noble, Norrie always knowing they were to miss the appointed ferry. Devious or what. It was probably to stop Peter messing with his territory, I guess!

Peter had a new company car with his new job and began driving in Holland at a relatively moderate speed after they caught a later ferry and were hopelessly late. Norrie, knowing it was a very long trip to Assen in the north of the country, said, "Pull over, I need a wee." But instead, Norrie jumped into the driver's seat and sped off at 100mph with his passengers, much to the consternation of Peter and his lovely new car, not now being gently run in.

John remembered driving on the way back and experiencing brake failure and shooting straight over one of the big Dutch roundabouts, luckily without harm to occupants or car.

Norrie had the annoying habit, after you'd told him of some hot breaking news, which you knew you were the first to get, and he couldn't possibly already know, would say, "Aye, ah know!" (yes, I know), very bluffly. Yes, Norrie, because I've just told you! Bless him.

Bob Berry was a very popular editor too, even for his "fashionable" permed hair during one period. Bob was hands-on and was a brilliant page designer; I've never seen anyone who could design a cracking, very special page in a newspaper as quickly as he could. He was probably better at the production side of editorial, but under his editorship, *MCN* continued on its lucrative, merry way, getting bigger and better. Front pages were particular sparkling under his reign.

Among the many brilliant reporters was Peter Howdle, always referred to as "Monsieur" in the office as he spoke fluent French, some of it learned when apparently living at a brothel, only as a bed and breakfast guest, I have to add! Monsieur had been a rear gunner in Lancaster bombers during the War, but he survived all his missions when many in that most vulnerable position didn't. We used to love his war stories when we could get him to talk about his experiences. I believe he and his RAF pals "imported" possibly the first VW Beetle car (Hitler's infamous "people's car") from Germany to the UK in a transport plane, but unfortunately for them, the commanding officer of the station saw it being wheeled out of the belly of the plane transporter, and he told them to take it back to Germany forthwith, which they had to comply with.

Peter had been one of *MCN*'s early editors in even more carefree days than those I enjoyed early on in my own *MCN* days. Once, suffering from a broken leg and broken arms, Peter was in hospital, and so that he could smoke his beloved cigarettes, he made up a series of metal rods, hinged so that he could light his fag and learnt to swing it upwards into his mouth. It was quite usual during my time at the office for the shout to go up from fellow colleagues, "Monsieur, your bin's on fire again," and quick action of foot stamping in the bin was required to stop a catastrophe. Only once did a fire engine have to be called to the offices, but it was not anything to do with Peter, it was smouldering computer wiring much later in *MCN*'s Station Road days which evacuated the building (including Dabbsy being carried safely down the stairways).

I believe it was also Peter, telling a story of an earlier time at *MCN* when what purported to be a tour of beautiful Yorkshire, Lake District or Dales by bike in the paper, was actually not what it seemed! A front wheel and set of forks were carried in the boot of a warm, heated, comfortable *MCN* staffer's car. Especially perhaps in mid-winter, the intrepid Peter or his cohorts used to drive the car, heater full on, and when photos were required, the "front" of the bike was lifted out and placed carefully on the edge of the frame of the photo, so that it looked as though the "rider" of the said bike, had just got off, and carefully framed his front wheel in the photo of the lovely, countryside view in a series of "best of countryside rides" by *MCN*. Naughty, but very resourceful, it has to be said. I bet it's never been admitted by the world's largest selling motorcycle paper! Whoops. Sorry, folks.

Thinking of smoking, not this time Peter Howdle, but our reporter Jerry Clayton, who smoked a pipe (as I did for a number of years), who was in charge of road tests. He loved any touring bike or sidecar with a high screen in those days, so that he could ride along with his pipe lit, although the hot ash was likely to singe his ginger beard in his open-face helmet.

He had the most astonishing high-pitched infectious laugh of anyone I have ever heard. Lovely man. Lovely company, as were many of the *MCN* staff reporters and sub-editors.

For many years, most of the editorial staff used to go down to a "greasy spoon" café in the cattle market, which was also a pub that never shut when the farmers came into town to sell their sheep and cows at auction. There was a fruit machine, bacon sarnies and beer and if our work was already done, "lunch hour" could spread well into the afternoon if Norrie had anything to do with it.

The beer and the café were just Norrie's type of place, more like his hometown of Dumfries, I reckon. It was a particularly free and easy life, and I am glad I enjoyed it while it was there because round the corner was coming "normal office routines", nine to five hours, and many, many, more, eating lunch at your desk (if you were a twat) and no elevenses breaks. You should have had breakfast before you came to work, said one later editor. But in the golden days, I remember seeing a particularly beautiful, full-on metallic Laser green Peugeot 206 GTI car and buying it in my lunch "hour". "Where have you been, Andrew?" asked Norrie when I reappeared mid-afternoon: "Oh, I've just been into town and bought a car." OK, then.

Another cracking editor was Adam Duckworth. A huge man, who in 2005 won a Slimmer of the Year award, losing 12 stone. A great feat.

Adam was a terrific rider on pedal bicycles and had the trickest lightweight one I'd seen. As well as being a first-rate journalist, and one of the quickest I've ever seen at writing a story, bar none, Adam was a top photographer. In later years he won Commercial Photographer of the Year award. Adam was a larger-than-life character who loved a laugh and in his time as editor, laughs were many, some very near the knuckle and some way past it.

Road race journo extraordinaire John Brown was the opposite of Adam when it came to writing to deadline. Nothing could be written by "Brownie" until the very, very last time for deadline of his copy. Then it was all panic and he would start bashing away, probably been in the pub till the last minute, then dashing back to write up his story. I can still hear him when he said, "How you doing, ace?" Everyone was "ace" to Brownie, including you, old son. John was a terrific reporter for *MCN*, and he too knew everyone in road racing, from the newest junior rookie rider to all the stars of the past and present. He was an encyclopaedia of road racing, jovial, larger than life and a great asset to *MCN*. Everyone knew Brownie. There'll never be another. He talked to anyone in road racing, from the novice club racer just starting out to the international heroes of the GP stars making the headlines of the days with their great exploits. It was his humble way. He made time for anyone, which is why his copy was always late, but it was a fabulous way to get stories. Him and his mate Dave the Bake had been in more pubs in Britain than any other pair, that's for sure. I'd bet money on that. A true legend in his own lunchtime was John as *Private Eye* famously said.

I worked with some very good sports editors too. Among them was Chris Herring – or "Kipper" to everyone at *MCN* – for obvious reasons.

Chris is a great journalist, very calm, very ordered, a good listener and a terrific writer. He had a stellar career at *MCN* before going into an even more illustrious position as team boss with Honda Racing Japan and their Moto GP team, working alongside the likes of Dani Pedrosa when the Honda giant was top of the circuits.

He was destined for the top was Chris because he had such brilliant journalistic ability. And his desk was as ordered as Norrie's too. But even cleaner because every week, out would come polish and a duster for a once over. Funny the little things that stick in your memory, while some bigger events, you have to look up.

Chris remains one of the organisers of the Friday 13th Club, which had as its founder in 1987, editor Bob Berry. Lunches have continued to be enjoyed in varied hostelries in Northamptonshire by many old *MCN* reporters for over 30 years, joined by many friends and guests from racing. Just some of the names have included Steve Parrish, Mick Hemmings, Colin Hill, Keith Huewen, Niall Mackenzie, Troy Bayliss, Charlie Rous, and speedway world champion Sam Ermolenko. Plus, *MCN* regulars, the late John Brown, the late John Phillips (advertising guru), Graham Sanderson, Stuart Barker, the late Jim Lindsay (editor), Chris Moss, Bob Berry, Paul Fowler, John Noble, Ron Pearson, Neil Webster, Chris Dabbs, Colin Hill and newcomers like me and sub-editor Tony Smith.

Rob McDonald was a very caring sports editor. He had great ability, knew his subject inside out and was very helpful and fair to me. When I left in 1996, I had lost my mother that year, so was in an odd place mentally and had made my decision to take early retirement. But it was Rob who fully understood what I was going through and asked me if I wanted to put off the decision and leave later. It was a very sympathetic ear and one I will always remember. But it did not put me off, and I took early retirement after 24 years of service and had got away without a heart attack, stroke or permanent deafness (just a touch of tinnitus) through standing too close to 14 speedway bikes being warmed up in the pits (especially the one at the concrete-enclosed Plough Lane Stadium, Wimbledon). Now another venue sadly demolished.

But there are other reminiscences of editors too. Marc Potter I only remember coming as a junior reporter, a very fresh-faced lad. He became the youngest editor at *MCN* and served for nine years (2003–2012). Amazing, I can still see Marc as that youth. He rose to become chief road tester, features editor and news editor at EMAP Automotive.

Rob Munro-Hall was another case altogether. He was appointed editor in 1990 and he didn't like me. I believe he picked on me, and the time comes when you think, editors are getting younger, you are getting older, and perhaps you are getting towards the end of your sell by date after so many years in the same game. Those were the vibes I was getting off Munro-Hall anyway. But he had a meteoric career. MD of EMAP's Bikes Division, Australian move in 2003 to launch *Zoo* and later Group MD Bauer Media. So his time at little ole *MCN* Kettering was not wasted on his career path. And I didn't hold him up.

Kevin Ash was an ace road tester at *MCN* and was a lovely chap with a very quick wit. His knowledge of bikes and the motorcycle industry was legendary, and I knew him at *MCN* in the 90s. He became a terrific, first-class freelancer, but was killed testing a BMW R1200GS in South Africa in 2013.

This might be a good place to say I was a road tester for *MCN* too. But not for me the super bikes we regularly road tested with their phenomenal horsepower and 150, 160, 170 mph-plus top speeds. I did the occasional 50 or 125! Ah well. One I remember was a new M reg Puch M50 sports moped, which looked every inch a bike to me anyway, until you spotted the pedals.

Don't laugh, but someone had to do it, the "sixteener" market was an essential one for the young rider coming into motorcycling under new laws. And this Puch was a beauty, having a good four-speed gearbox, a good seat and a proper riding position. The photo of me in *MCN* riding the little bike showed me in an open-face helmet and goggles and a two-piece nylon suit (which if I remember was red). Maximum speed was 45mph, which was pretty good for a 50cc moped. Our test bike blew both its bulbs and the spring fell off the stand while it was with us, I reported.

Yes, it's me on a little Puch, a picture that appeared in
MCN. Someone had to do the road test!

I also knew Andy Calton on his first employment at *MCN*. I knew him as a trainee sub-editor and he too was a quick learner. So much so that after gaining much experience in journalism at *MCN* and in the golfing world, he became editor of the newspaper in 2012, his third stint at *MCN*. He also helped launch *MCNSport* and *MCNBikeMart* before he became editor. He still went occasionally for a night at Peterborough speedway, where *MCN* resides, with some of his staff for a bike ride out.

Sub-editor Jack Scott had worked on *New Musical Express* before his employment at the office. Good sub too. His best story about his tenure at *NME* was of a very young David Bowie, then unknown, who kept coming into the music paper's editorial offices and made such a nuisance of himself, presumably just getting in the way, he was told by the editorial team to "f...k off!" I've dined out on my David Bowie story many times.

There were also tragedies along the way as well. *MCN* lost a very fine young editor, Peter Bolt, who was killed on a bike on his way back home to Northampton after putting his paper to "bed" after a press day in 1992. I was going to Peterborough speedway for their press launch early the next day when I heard the news of his death on the local radio. I wanted to verify the story and rang the office, and Norrie Whyte was taking all calls, and there must have been hundreds that morning, who sadly told me it was true. We were all devastated at losing our chief, the man who was pretty much cheerful all the time and rose to become a mighty fine editor of biking's flagship title. One of *MCN*'s best.

It was a time for personal reflection. I had shared with Peter some of my personal problems, and despite his being much younger than I, he too had a sympathetic ear, which helped enormously. I remember the funeral now, there wasn't a dry eye in the place, remembering such a lovely, young, family man. Peter was a lively chap, ex-punk, who certainly had a mischievous way about him, and I think he had his own way of thinking about things. He was an outstanding newspaperman, very knowledgeable on his subject, approachable, fair, and a terrific ideas man and a good friend at *MCN*.

Maybe now is a good time to try to explain how *MCN* gathered its sports reports nationwide every weekend for the paper which came out on Wednesdays. There was a posse of intrepid correspondents all over the country, from Scotland, Wales, Ireland and each English county in between. The posse was controlled by Norrie Whyte, who gave his "orders" each week to his men and women correspondents. It was Norrie who would say to each correspondent he wanted them to write 50 words on some trial that weekend, 100 words on a motocross, 200 words on a road race meeting. Photos from another meeting, etc. This was done all over the country, and it was this army of people, arranged by Norrie, which gave *MCN* its superiority over any other publication at that time.

Our coverage of all motorcycle events throughout the country was amazing. Although termed a comic by some, it was also thought of as a bible by others, especially by centre competitors, who if they got their name in *MCN* for finishing say sixth in race two of the Dilly Dally scramble in Cumbria, thought it absolutely thrilling, which it was to them. And a service provided only by *MCN* and its hardworking, knowledgeable correspondents in every county in the land.

Sunday nights were a bit special at *MCN*. Copy typists from the local area were recruited and worked maybe from 7 till around midnight or beyond. It was their job to take down all the copy created by our army of correspondents on mechanical typewriters – no computers or internet then, we thought the fax machine was the very best in high technology in those days. Until the darn thing jammed or ran out of paper, especially if it ran out of paper at night while it should be taking copy from far-flung places like America or Australia.

I think there were perhaps half a dozen young women who came in to do their "shift" at *MCN* in those far-off days. They were often young mothers who could only earn some money on Sunday evenings when their husbands could look after the children at home. Most of them were very bright people; the "whingers" didn't last long. Many reports from abroad would come on the fax machine, and they too had to be put into *MCN* style by our office staff, often by the fantastic Pat, a county championship swimmer. *MCN*'s fax machine was definitely the hardest working one in Kettering. Dozens and dozens of reports of foreign championships came in each Sunday night from across the world. Paper running out at critical times, inks running out were regular perils, mixed in with mechanical breakdowns and paper jams!

Dozens of championships had to be updated after each event, each week, which was a horrible job, but always done immaculately by Pat. A staff of sub-editors were in each Sunday night for a shift, and it was their job to make sense of the contributors' copy, often from motorcycle enthusiasts who were not journalists, so difficult to get into newspaper English! Bless them all. It was this coverage of all the small sporting events throughout the land which made *MCN* unique. And if we didn't put in the results of their events, then there was hell to pay from the secretary of the meeting on Wednesday, publication day.

On a Sunday night, *MCN* staff men would be coming in from the major events that they had been to that day, could be a road race from Germany, a trial in Spain, a motocross in the Netherlands, and even a speedway meeting or two. Some events were too far to get flights back for Sunday nights, so much quick writing from the reporters went on into "press day" each Monday.

But back to Sunday. Photos came in from national events and they were all then black-and-white negative film rolls, none of your digital stuff. We used to use darkroom staff from the local *Evening Telegraph* newspaper to do the developing of films. I've said it before, but some who work constantly with developing chemicals in darkrooms become decidedly odd! I'm sure it affects the way their brains act. Some seemed just odd people. Like a *County Express* photographer who said it was impossible to take pictures at swimming galas. Full stop. Would never go to one.

Not like our brilliant freelance contributing lensmen, some of the best in the land, including former *MCN* staff man Don Morley, who continued to send in his superb photos, along with the likes of Jim Greening, Brian Holder, Malcolm Carling, Wright Wood, Alf Weedon, John Sumpter, Mike Kilby and Cecil Bailey and many, many more.

Packages of photos would also arrive in Kettering from all over the land from couriers who had been organised to bring us event pictures from abroad after taking packages off aircraft at all the big airports. Everything, copy and photos had to be done mechanically, without mobile phones etc. All had to be written down on bits of paper. And don't forget, we were still using Victorian technology of hot metal printing presses after it had been stacked into galleys; each story made up of single lines of letters stamped in lead. Marvellous, and I am glad I lived through it all and took my very small part in such a wonderful industry.

Walking alongside a press, taller than a double-decker bus and a hundred feet long, churning out newspapers from giant reels of paper, with your words you have written somehow incorporated into them, can only be described as mind-bogglingly magic. As the whole paper was put together as an issue, it was just great to be able to pull one copy out of the machine as it spewed completed *MCN*s on a Tuesday after you'd worked at an event on Saturday or Sunday, worked Sunday night, a full press day on Monday. Well over 100,000 copies on all the news-stands across the country on a Wednesday.

Digital publishing? Wonderful. But not my kind of publishing. An era gone. Like the dinosaurs. I was one.

Chapter 12

Peter Arnold nostalgia

Before *MCN* editor Peter Strong edited the speedway pages in *MCN*, they employed an extraordinary journalist to look after speedway for them. He was Peter Arnold, who had lived in Pipewell, the next village to where I lived in Rushton, Northamptonshire.

Peter Arnold was not even his real name, but his "stage name". He had been born Alan Baxter. He adopted his name Peter Arnold and produced stage shows while in the RAF. He commentated on road race circuits as well as speedway and hot rods and rose to become assistant editor of *Motor Cycle News*. Peter commentated on speedway right up to World Finals at Wembley. He was the greatest self-publicity machine in the world too. If his name appeared in any publication, just a line, he'd cut it out and paste it in scrapbooks, which to this day, I still have. Unfortunately, he died of a heart attack driving back from a speedway meeting at Reading after his duties as track speedway announcer in 1969. He was returning home to near where I lived and wrote part of this book.

I found albums of old speedway photos (collected by a fan I think) going right back to the start of the sport in the 1920–30s up to the 50s in tea chests ready for the tip in the bike garage at *MCN*, and I asked if I could rescue them, and the answer was yes. Any speedway programme (just the cover, unfortunately) was kept with Peter's name in as track announcer, any annual dinner menus, after-dinner speeches, *TV Times* and *Radio Times* cuttings when he appeared discussing motorcycle matters were collected. He kept them all in his own cuttings' library. Even the letter congratulating him for his work as announcer at the 1962 Wembley World Final. It was a special one, with the late Peter Craven winning his second world crown. The letter from the Speedway Control Board to P Arnold Esq, Motorcycle News, Dryland Street, Kettering, Northants reads: "Dear Peter, re Wembley 8th September. I enclose Control Board cheque for 4 guineas, being your fee for the above meeting. Whilst writing, may I congratulate you on the way you carried out the job – which was, of course, only to be expected."

It was Peter who started the Veteran Dirt Track Riders Association, first called the Pioneer Dirt Track Riders Association, in 1957. It is now still going strong as the World Speedway Riders Association, of which I am an associate member. He was association secretary in 1957–58 and laid down the principles of the Veteran's group "to be purely social or benevolent in character, not to interfere in the government of the sport." The list of people who have served as President of the Association reads like a who's who of speedway and includes Frank Varey, Gus Kuhn, Phil Bishop, Wal Phillips, Squib Burton, Jack Parker, Johnnie Hoskins,

Tiger Hart, Fred Williams, Jack Milne, Eric Boothroyd, Reg Fearman, Ove Fundin, Barry Briggs, Vic White, Ronnie Moore, Ivan Mauger and Bert Harkins.

Bert Harkins at Golden Greats, Coventry, a terrific performer for Scottish speedway over many years. One of very few spectacle-wearing riders, now championing the World Speedway Riders Association.

Peter was a man of many parts. I am sure he had, like me, a sense of history for the sport which should be properly documented before important bikes, equipment and all artefacts are lost to future generations. To this end, Peter had the idea of the first speedway museum, which was set up at the Beaulieu Montague Museum in May 1957 after Peter had met Lord Montagu at a speedway meeting. Members of Southampton Saints team put on the club colours once again for the occasion;

Brian Hanham, Bill Holden, Maurice Mattingley and Alby Golden gave demonstrations on a specially laid out "track". It got a bit out of hand, for veteran Phil Bishop went out of control and disappeared into a daffodil flowerbed, only to reappear a bit red faced in front of the Lord of the Manor! The museum was opened on May 12 and was open every day during the summer months and on weekends during the winter. To follow in the footsteps of such a speedway icon as Peter Arnold was for me a great honour.

But it proved not to be a permanent museum, which was also the fate of the next speedway museum. Barry Briggs and Tom Wheatcroft, the owner of Donington Park racetrack in Leicestershire, opened the next one, although they said they were the first, in 1988.

The speedway Hall of Fame was an excellent representation of all things speedway and stood alongside the marvellous collection of Wheatcroft's historic Formula One cars. But that closed when the space was needed for more cars.

The present excellent museum is at Paradise Wildlife Park, White Stubbs Lane, Broxbourne, Herts. And the World Speedway Riders' Association and Friends of Speedway honours the memory of the greats of the sport with tribute plaques too. They do an excellent job.

But the man who helped me at *MCN* more than anyone else was Peter Oakes. As a brilliant journalist and successful speedway promoter at many venues,

Peter fed me all the up-to-date news stories for many, many years, as he had done in the past for editor "Strongy". He was a great servant and helper to me and to *MCN* for a very long time, and without his help, I simply couldn't have done what I did as a wet behind the ear's "rookie". It was more often than not his copy that made headline news in *MCN* and *Speedway Star* as well as the national papers, which then showed a great interest in speedway, as opposed to now when it is virtually ignored as the sport got smaller and more parochial. He worked for American and Australian magazines and was manager to Ivan Mauger for many years, publishing Ivan's annuals, books and working as his PRO. His speedway works of reference included the *Speedway Yearbooks*, the *Complete History of the British League* and *Who's Who of World Speedway*. Peter also edited Tai Woffinden's bestselling book. Peter had another career as well; he was showbusiness reporter and TV columnist for the *Sunday People* too and was a Hugh Cudlipp Award winner for his showbusiness coverage in the national paper in 1975.

It was one of the great privileges to work alongside most of the sport's greats during my time at *MCN* and afterwards too. Such memories.

Chapter 13

Fan to speedway reporter

That was me then, starting out as a fan, a supporter and progressing to a working journalist with *MCN*, which gave unprecedented access to leading officials, the decision makers, the referees, clerks of the course, promoters, the movers and shakers at the British Speedway Promoters' Association and the top-level bosses and rule makers at the FIM, and not least, the people who really mattered, the riders themselves. What a journey.

As members of the British press, we had almost unlimited access to the riders. As long as you used your common sense and approached them when they were obviously not busy doing other things, the co-operation from the top men was terrific. Ivan Mauger was the one who stands out. You had to get his trust; he definitely was one who didn't suffer fools at all! But over the seasons, I think he trusted me, and when the mighty man had won his sixth world title in Chorzow, Poland in 1979, he was so relaxed he simply hitched a lift with the press who were being taken back to the hotel in a coach and sat next to me.

I didn't waste the opportunity and "interviewed" him as we sat together. I did not get my notebook out as I thought it might interrupt his flow, and instead after the short ride back simply went straight to somewhere quiet to remember and transcribed everything I could quickly, so as not to forget a thing. I thought the feature on Ivan in the following week's *MCN* was OK. Another job done.

Me, left, with Ivan Mauger, centre, and Ole Olsen. 1979 World Final practice, Chorzow, Poland. 24 hours later, Ivan won his sixth World Championship.

MCN loved their rider columnists, and many top stars of speedway were involved over the years. Some like John Louis's columns were great because he sent them in for publication ready typed up. A real star and a gentleman, who still lied to me when I did a feature on him while standing in the centre green at Mildenhall speedway during a training session he was running! He was a lot older than he let on when he turned to speedway after a glittering motocross career and simply took years off his real age! It was Peter Oakes who in later years found John's real age and he was "outed"!

Others were, shall we say, a little bit more difficult to get to grips with! The prime example was Nigel Boocock. He had a great sense of humour, but a lot of what he thought would make interesting reading in his by-lined column was not fit for print; shall we just say too rude and leave it at that! Trying to track him down was sometimes a nightmare for me, especially when he was on one of his regular winter tours with the British Lions in Australia. The itinerary took him all over Australia, and of course there was the time difference and Nigel's complete lack of urgency and his work as rider and captain of the team.

I do not know what the calls cost to speak to Nigel, but they must have been horrendously expensive. Still, we got the columns and all the up-to-date news of the Lions' triumphs and disasters straight from the riders' point of view, and they were very useful in filling space when racing was not being held in the winter in the UK. Great winter copy with excellent photos from Down Under too. Also, still no mobile phones, so keeping tabs on "Little Boy Blue" (because of his trademark blue leathers) was a nightmare.

At Nigel's home in Coventry, I went along and met his wife, Cynthia, to do a feature on him. Sometimes an hour or two is sufficient, but Nigel had me for the day. I remember we went to see his wheel builder nearby and all sorts of little trips like that. All very interesting and gave me a nice background to what a top international rider did in preparations for meetings. I remember he swore blind on using vitamin E extract for getting bruises out after his many crashes during a long and brilliant career.

It was time for a photo shoot on the back lawn with a bike wheeled out and Nigel posing on it with an England body colour on. He insisted on holding a small, furry round thing, which after I'd handled it, he told me was the dried testicle case of an Australian kangaroo! He thought it hilarious. That was just one example of Nigel's off-the-wall sense of humour that day and possibly the only one fit for publication. Nigel was a brilliant, courageous rider who had his fair share of big knocks, but I will always remember him as a great friend to *MCN* who always helped us and me out. He always championed *MCN* and was very loyal to us. He and his England team which toured and took on Australia in the off-season for many years were once equipped with blue and white *MCN* anoraks. Very proud he was of that, I remember.

It was that feature on Nigel in November 1974 when one of my own photos appeared in *MCN*. Not with the testicle case this time, but on the back lawn on a speedway bike, surrounded by Union Jack body colours hanging on the fence, all gold-edged, meaning they were World Final jackets. He rode in World Finals as a qualifier eight times and was a reserve twice. In 1969, he finished on 10 points for fourth place, his highest position. He rode for England 55 times, Great Britain 54 times and the British Lions 59 times.

Nigel told me then: "I may not be a millionaire, but I've got a few quid! Speedway has enabled me to see the world and meet a hell of a lot of nice people, although there are some mongrels in speedway as well. I wouldn't swop it looking back."

He had his fair share of knocks did Booey, including a skull fracture which saw him unconscious for about a week. But he always bounced back to continue his full-bore style, right to the end of his career. During his 20-year riding span, Nigel had only been associated with four tracks (this was in 1974), and the first three closed down! It is sadly ironic that the track which saw out the greatest part of his career, Coventry, since his death, has now also closed.

He said he'd come a long way since he got married and lived in a caravan on the Ipswich car park. Nigel said: "The first time I ever rode a speedway bike was when I borrowed one for £3 to have a belt round the Newton Heath training track run by Ernie Appleby. He started me off really, set the ball rolling. I rode the training bike about three times, and then they told me I would get further if I bought my own bike. So I did. I bought one for £65 with financial assistance from my mother and father. I will never forget my first competitive speedway race. It was in the second half of a meeting at Belle Vue, Manchester. I made the first corner and wham, I fell off. I was 16 years old then.

"After that I went to Bradford and won my first race! But after that, I fell off in every meeting for four or five weeks until I really clobbered the fence at Whitsun and broke my nose, jaw, collarbone, two ribs and was unconscious for six days. That was the end of my first season in speedway!

"I couldn't afford to be a road racer, but I wanted to race motorcycles and the only thing that I could afford to do which would pay me from my first race was speedway. No other motorcycle sport (even now) can do this. To start in scrambling for instance you need to buy a £600 bike (in 1974) to be competitive with big prize money only paid to the stars. In speedway, every rider gets paid the same."

In the 1974 feature, Nigel said: "Some of the differences I have noticed over 20 years are changes in track surfaces and a great change in engine and frame designs. The tracks are now as hard as concrete, and you have to detune engines to get grip."

I ended the story entitled "Twenty Years On" by saying, "He has been a good servant to speedway and has always shown great sportsmanship. It will be hard to replace a man like that."

His career record started in Bradford in 1955, then moved to Birmingham, Ipswich, Coventry (1959–1976), Bristol, Exeter, Canterbury and Swindon.

Many, many years later, it was great to meet up with Nigel again, who had emigrated to Australia, at a Barry

Briggs Golden Greats meeting at Coventry and have some photos taken with him and Ove Fundin, which I still have. More treasured memories. It was a terrible blow when Nigel died in 2015. What a rider. His memorial at Coventry speedway, when Peter Collins went round the track on Boocock's trusty bike with his ashes on board, drew more people perhaps than a normal Elite League match of that time.

Brother Eric was very different to Nigel. His equal as a top rider, but more serious in trying to do his best to change speedway for the better. He became a great friend to me, and his phone calls to me at the office sometimes went on for hours. Eric was good for "copy", only beaten by Simon Wigg. If I hadn't got a good story that day, it was a case of I'll just ring Wiggy or Eric and more often than not, they would come up with a little gem of a story right off the cuff! Or know someone who could sort me out a big story for *MCN* headlines.

But back to Eric. He did sterling service for his clubs, won the British championship with a very bad arm injury which ended his shale career and did a brave job later as England team manager along with Colin Pratt. It was always a difficult position to be in, trying to juggle the politics and keep all promoters happy while picking the best teams for the job. He could talk speedway for England could Booey and we got on well. It was while Eric held the British championship trophy that I noticed there was an error on the cup; championship was spelt wrong and still is.

Years before I joined *MCN*, I was at Coventry watching a match when Booey became mightily upset at being thrown out of a race after the referee had looked at a review of the start on a TV screen and Eric had placed his bike across the track at the tapes so the race couldn't start. The photo which was used in the papers, with Eric and the bike at the tapes, clearly has me and my friends in the crowd in the background, watching proceedings. Trial by television said Eric and was unlawful because not all referees had the chance to look at TV screen recordings if meetings weren't televised.

Another *MCN* columnist, Barry Briggs, was involved with me in trying to prove that his dirt deflector, which was being tried out to stop shale from going over the fence and into the crowds, really worked to make it a safer, health and safety environment for the fans. We had Cradley Heath stadium to ourselves for the day, and I had come up with the idea of using some clean, giant white newspaper end of reels, which looked like big cotton reel holders, unravelled and pinned onto the fence, so that we could actually record how high the shale went with and without dirt deflectors in a controlled experiment. I think it was Steve Bastable who rode round for us, and we did indeed prove that the dirt deflectors were environmentally friendly and did stop a lot of shale going over the fence into the crowd. You could see the marks of the shale as it hit the paper and the marks were a lot higher without the dirt deflector fitted to Steve's bike as he rode round on the same line entering the bend for us in a before and after test. And dirt deflectors are now part and parcel of speedway and are used everywhere worldwide.

Barry Briggs, left, and I taking down hundreds of yards of end-of-reel newspaper print which we pinned to the fence for a dirt deflector test at Cradley speedway. The dirt deflector soon afterwards became compulsory to stop shale flying over the fence into spectators' areas.

Briggo later became the first speedway rider to appear on TV's *This is Your Life* programme while he was still an active participant. The presenter of the show, Eamon Andrews, dressed up as a track grader at Wimbledon stadium to surprise Briggo with the famous red book after he pulled onto the centre green after some "demo" laps. Guests included Ivan Mauger, Ronnie Moore and Ove Fundin, who honoured the four-times world champion. Another first for speedway.

Barry Sheene was later another "victim" of presenter Andrews and his red book when he was surprised at a motorcycle show in London, and he too was whisked off to the studio for another episode of *This is Your Life*. And I was among the audience for the filming. Very hot it was too under those studio lights. I am sure though that Barry went along with the surprise; I'm sure he already knew! He was too cute to be caught out I reckon.

Chapter 14

MCN on tour, to Silverstone GP

It was not all speedway at *MCN*. I got to meet some of the top road racers, motocross and trials men. One of the annual treats for me for a few years was the visit to Silverstone for the British Motorcycle Grand Prix.

Our chief reporter Norrie Whyte found an ingenious way of beating the huge traffic jams by hiring an old caravan for the *MCN* editorial to base themselves in at the track. This was towed to the circuit for Norrie and placed behind the fans' campsite. It was a brilliant scheme involving John Brown, ace road race reporter, "Dave the Bake" who was a baker (of course) and a great friend of John's, me, and a huge stew, and I mean huge, made by Norrie's wife at the time, Doreen, who was a domestic science teacher and a very good cook. She used to make up an enormous casserole which served us for the entire weekend. It was in a vast stockpot, and my job was to keep it upright in the car on the floor between my knees, it was far too precious for the boot in case it toppled over. I think if I'd spilt it, they'd have had my guts for garters, and we would have all gone hungry!

I don't think we actually had it for breakfast, but it was heated up in the caravan when people wanted food during Friday night, Saturday and I suppose even Sunday. It must have been a big un! I know it was glorious, lovely grub. And certainly beat Silverstone's greasy burger and chips, high cholesterol, near heart-attack menu. One year, some of the fans got a little boisterous and I heard one of the biggest bangs I'd ever heard in my life. Some lunatic had thrown a big empty Calor gas container onto a campfire and it had exploded. Luckily, I heard of no injuries.

It was the 70s and the glory days for road racing too. To see Barry Sheene, world champion in the 1976 race at Silverstone with Kenny Roberts was terrific and we had the best view in the house. With our infield passes, we were able to drive cars between the best bends to get right up close to the action. Incidentally, 1976 was definitely the year of the Brits, with Sheene world road race champ, Peter Collins world speedway champ and James Hunt, F1 world champion. What a year and what a year to be involved in motorcycle race reporting if you were British.

One of my small "claims to fame" was being in the same motorcycle programme as Barry Sheene when he was world champion in 1976! But only in a trial. *MCN* helped organise an annual Wayzgoose press trial in the woods at the back of Brands Hatch road race circuit. A lot of top riders, friends who helped *MCN* were invited, and it was a party day out with *MCN* reporters of all ages and different standards of trials riding. I was absolutely, totally rubbish and a bit petrified of the hairy sections and gave most of them a miss on a borrowed 250 Suzuki one year, I remember, keeping me and the bike clean and out of the worst of the mud holes. Even going to the start, I was giving *MCN* reporter John "Ace" Brown a lift on the rear mudguard and he shouted in a tremulous voice, "Has this thing got any more gears?" I was riding it with maximum revs in first gear to get to the first section across the Brands car park, forgetting, with my cargo, it had other gears too.

To get things in context, also riding in the programme was Barry's lovely wife Steph and his dad Frank, all on Bultacos!

Incidentally, Barry would do everything he could by ringing round various members of the *MCN* editorial team to find out if he'd won the coveted *MCN* Man of the Year award, voted for by our readers. He used to threaten not to turn up at the Lyceum Ballroom, London, for the big night of the year when the awards were announced if he hadn't won! As the main man, everyone's hero, he did win it, I think, five times between 1973 and 1979. (Peter Collins, our speedway man, was runner-up in the readers' poll back in his world title year, 1976.) Barry was runner-up in 1974, 1978, 1980, 1981.

I did get better on my own beloved Honda SL125 trail bike than at the Brands press trial and had many lovely rides in the Northants countryside. Finding disused railway tracks was a great idea because you could ride along the paths (without the railway lines, of course) quite quickly, to me anyway. One day, I and Brian "Badger" Crichton, *MCN* reporter and later classics editor, on his 250 Honda trail bike, found a wooden bridge that had big holes in it.

My favourite bike, my own Honda SL125 trail.
As they say, wish I'd kept it too!

We had to dismount, manoeuvre our bikes on one plank of wood which looked safe-ish and walk alongside the bikes on another plank, not looking down at the ground quite some way below. Quite dodgy, looking back! I know owners always say this, but I do wish I still had that little 125 Honda trail bike. It looked superb, ran like a Swiss watch and started every time, first kick. Good for road trips and the occasional green lane. I had many of my own bikes during my lifetime. I started out on a Triumph Tina, an automatic. I fell off it first day I had it, ripped my trousers, and passed my test on it, too, when I stopped falling off it. I had a Honda S90 which was a super little bike and with a full fairing on it, which would pull 60mph plus, two up. Loving Hondas, I went up to an electric start Honda 150 twin in red (which got sold for my first car). Then came the Honda SL125 trail bike, while at *MCN*, followed by a buzzy MZ250 "flying banana", named because of the shape of its tank. It was a particular favourite of readers of *Motorcycle Sport*, and that's why I got sucked into buying one, I think, but I'm afraid I didn't get on with it at all, especially as the headlight didn't turn with the 'bars, but was fixed instead to the one-piece tank etc. Very odd! Then came a Yamaha 100 or 125 two-stroke which I bought from a fellow journalist in the *MCN* office, but I did not use it very often. It was Belfast, Northern Ireland registered and to make it legal, I had to re-register it in the DVLA at Northampton.

Chapter 15

Back to the speedway

Back to the speedway. 1978 was the Golden Jubilee year of British speedway, which had arrived in this country at High Beech in 1928, although other venues have good claims to have run the first meeting in the UK. But it was Danish champion Ole Olsen who spoilt the party at Wembley when he won, with Gordon Kennett, in his World Final debut, upholding England's honours that year with a superb second place in front of nearly 90,000 spectators. But for a small engine part, worth pennies, which failed in his first ride, it was said that Dave Jessup could have been world champion that year. He reeled off three wins among his 11 points which led him to finish fourth overall. Behind Kennett in third place was the charismatic American Scott Autrey, so nearly a world champion, he had the proven abilities, but who never quite made the top spot in a glittering career, most of it played out in Britain. An intelligent, top rider, who deserved a world title.

The Golden Jubilee anniversary was celebrated with a special meeting at Hackney and was the only time I saw legendary Jack Parker ride in a special match race with Malcolm Simmons, which Jack "won" although he was on a "modern" machine and Simmo on a dirt track Rudge, or something similar, in very much a demonstration race of course. We did get to see the founder of speedway, Johnnie Hoskins, have his hat set on fire, which had been a long-standing tradition in his career (not when he was wearing it of course) by rival teams, riders and promoters. Hoskins was master of the publicity stunt and never missed a trick at any of the tracks where he promoted during his long career, right up to his old age.

1978 was also the year I was proud to be an inaugural member of the newly formed Speedway Riders and Photographers Association (SWAPA). It all came about in a bar in Landshut, Germany, where I was reporting on the World Team Cup Final.

Seated in the bar that night were representatives, if I recall correctly, including the *Daily Express*, *Daily* and *Sunday Mirror*, *Sun*, *Daily Mail*, *Daily Star*, *Sunday Express*, *MCN*, *The Motor Cycle*, *Speedway Star*, *Speedway Mail* plus journalists from provincial newspapers.

That's how important speedway was to national newspapers then, they sent staff men to cover international speedway! We had the brainwave to form ourselves into an official organisation to represent the British speedway press. This would ease the always tricky registration for and collection of press passes to some continental tracks, where they never seemed to want to let any member of the foreign press in, who were only trying to do their jobs.

At the core of the organisation was Phil Rising, then editor of the *Speedway Star*, who always argued long and hard on behalf of his fellow journalists with reluctant organisers of major international speedway events. SWAPA also grew to organise many super gala dinners, attended by members from all over the world as the organisation went global, together with all the top riders and administrators of the sport, when a SWAPA Rider of the Year trophy was awarded, donated by *Vintage Speedway Magazine* publisher Peter Lipscomb. There were trophies for Administrator of the Year and Newcomer of the Year. Bruce Penhall won the 78 Newcomer trophy, so we got that one right at the start of one of the most glamorous careers in speedway, culminating in his double World Championship wins. SWAPA ties were issued to members, I still have mine, but alas SWAPA is no more. Gone, but not forgotten.

This is a SWAPA sticker printed for the association to help speedway reporters worldwide.

A SWAPA trip, Germany from left, back row: me,
Peter Lipscomb (*Vintage* magazine), Dick Bott (BBC Radio
Manchester), Mike Patrick, *Speedway Star* photographer,
Stewart Burroughs (*Motor Cycle*), Phil Rising, Paul Parish,
both *Speedway Star*. Front row: Mike Beale (*Daily Star*),
Keir Radnedge (*Daily Mail*), Graham Baker (*Daily Mirror*).

It was in that year gangly Englishman Michael Lee
burst onto the World Final scene. He scored nine
points to finish seventh in the 1978 World Final. Next
year, in 1979, Cambridge born Lee was on the rostrum
in third place at Chorzow, Poland, behind Ivan Mauger
and Zenon Plech, after he won a four-man run-off from
Kelly Moran, Billy Sanders and Ole Olsen. 1980 was to
be Lee's glory year. The year that England stood tall at
the top of the World Championship pile when Lee won
in Gothenburg, Sweden, in September of that year. I
had a pits' pass for the meeting and so was not in the
stands with the rest of the British press, which gave me

the great pleasure of saying congratulations to the King's Lynn star in the pits before almost anyone else, including any of the other scribes, after he won the title. It was a double celebration for England that year, with Dave Jessup in second spot after a run-off with Billy Sanders when both had scored 12 points. But it was Lee who scored two more points than either of them to become England's new world champion. A very great day for British speedway and Michael.

Mike Patrick had spotted a good photo opportunity in practice as rock group Supertramp were giving a concert in Gothenburg and popped into the stadium. Mike got a photo of Michael Lee with the group, and I took away a copy of their latest LP (those big black vinyl things) and no, I didn't get it signed either! That LP is still in my collection of ageing albums.

I do remember having to put the record under my coat to keep it dry from the Gothenburg rain while getting into a taxi after the meeting to get back to my hotel to write up the story. A very drunk Swede was getting into all sorts of problems trying to get into this taxi, and I don't think the taxi driver was impressed that he might have to take this drunk home, so I quickly stepped in and politely said, "Ramada Hotel?" to the driver. He obviously thought I was a safer bet and left his countryman still trying to sort himself out on the pavement!

I was the first national journalist to do a feature for *MCN* on Lee in 1975 as he turned 16, left school and signed for King's Lynn's First Division team, having started as a novice that same year with Boston Barracudas in the New National League. I remember visiting his home, taking a photo of him on a 50cc Kreidler Florett restricted sixteener moped, the only bike Lee could ride legally on the road, when he was already barnstorming British speedway on his 500cc steed. I remember his bad teeth (he was scared of dentists), which England team manager John Berry was instrumental in having sorted out. I took a photo of Michael on his front lawn with the moped and ripped flared trousers. Now that would be a cracker from the archives, but I don't have a copy, only the newspaper cutting. It was the start of a glorious career for Lee.

I wrote at the time: "In his first fantastic year he dented many an established star's reputation and in the recent Pride of the East meeting at his home (King's Lynn) track he scored 12 points, beating 1974 world champion Anders Michanek, British Lions tourist Dave Morton, world star Tommy Jansson, his own skipper Terry Betts and former British champion Ray Wilson."

Talking to Terry Betts, King's Lynn and England star man
and one of the nicest men in speedway I ever met.
Very talented rider amongst many of that era.

For me, he was simply the most natural rider ever to
have sat on a speedway machine, despite his long legs
making him really too tall to be a speedway rider. But
boy, could he ride, and it was a great shame for British
speedway, but more for him as a human being, that he
let himself down so badly later on when he simply
became speedway's bad boy. A prison sentence for drug
offences followed, and he swore to me after coming
out that he'd learnt his lesson. And I believed him. But
his bad habits brought him into bad company again
and he spent a second term locked up. He remained a
good friend, there was no point in judging him harshly.
He was intelligent enough to know he had done wrong
and admitted it. It was simply, I believe, too much

pressure on a young man's shoulders too early. He was speedway's George Best, the Irishman who had so many problems outside his talent at football. Talented beyond any normal person's dreams but fragile when it came to the temptations of life and having a good time, but not knowing when to draw a line.

Getting the lowdown of the race from world champion Michael Lee during an *MCN* Golden Helmet match race.

Later, Michael Lee got back on track with a highly successful tuning business and as promoter at National League Mildenhall Fen Tigers. Not many riders went to Cradley and could ride the pants off Bruce Penhall, but M Lee did it very regularly during his visits to Dudley Wood Stadium I seem to remember.

A short but spectacular career, and I am still privileged to say that I saw him race so marvellously and so spectacularly and will always remember shaking his hand at his great success in being the sport's number one in Sweden in 1980. Nobody can take his World Championship win from him. Wonderful memories of a genius, on a bike that is, but a genius nevertheless, albeit a flawed one. The original "wild child", indeed.

Bruce Penhall was one who was to change speedway forever during his tenure as the leading man in the sport. As he rode for Cradley Heath, starting in 1978 (through to 1982), I got to know him well, and was able to talk to him in the pits at Dudley Wood each Saturday. The word charisma is used too much in sport these days, but Bruce had charisma to spare! He was a god to the young girl fans with his California background, his good looks and blond hair! But with Bruce it was not all about hype, he underlaid the whole persona by being an exceptionally talented rider and nice guy.

The Americans brought huge changes, some good, some not so good, in world speedway. But Bruce was one of the best riders ever to come from America and he put thousands of bums on seats during his wonderful career in Britain. His tenure at Cradley gave them some of the most notable championship winning seasons they ever had.

Chapter 16

Cradley days

Life changed at little Cradley. They had always been the bridesmaid, never the bride until the likes of Bruce were attracted to the club and success like they'd never experienced before started to come to the Black Country, and the club became one of the big players in British speedway for many years after so many seasons in the wilderness. Crowds were always huge on Saturday nights at Cradley, and although there were many First Division football clubs in the Midlands (Aston Villa, Birmingham, West Bromwich Albion and Wolverhampton), talk in the pubs in and around the Cradley and Cradley Heath areas was always about the Heathens and what they had done that week. I tried to never miss a meeting and often stood next to promoter Derek Pugh in the pits, who had his own little footstool grandstand to give him a better view of the racing! So, he was always higher up than me by a foot or two and everyone else!

Bruce was the beating heart of the club during his time at Cradley. He drove them on to a new era of success, with the management making the club into a formidable league and knockout cup-winning machine. Led by Bruce, Cradley won their first British

League title in 1981, followed by another in 1983. He led the averages in the team in 81, which included Erik Gundersen, Alan Grahame, Phil Collins, David Shields, Bent Rasmussen and John McNeill, guided by brilliant manager Pete Adams. Bruce was not a typical loud Californian, he was a bit quieter, although he knew how to party alright, but he was always so professional in his dealings with the press boys, both at home and representing his country internationally. The record book shows Cradley were Knockout Cup winners in 1979, 1980, 1983, 1987,1988, 1989, League Cup winners in 1982, 1984, 1986 shared, Inter League Cup winners in 1979 and Premiership winners in 1982, 1985 and 1990. Apologies if I missed anything. I probably have!

The record books also show that Bruce won the last ever World Final staged at Wembley Stadium in 1981. One of the very best finals ever too. It marked the end of an era when Wembley always ran the largest speedway meeting on the planet under those iconic Twin Towers. Those great days of destiny were gone after that Final. What a meeting it was, many say the best Wembley-staged World Final of all, with Bruce winning on 14 points from Ole Olsen, second, and Tommy Knudsen, third. Bruce was Cradley's first world champion, and the fans went wild on the terraces chanting for their Juicy Brucie. Some of the racing is still talked about today. It was just so good. The fans were euphoric. The quality sublime.

With Bruce Penhall, one of speedway's most charismatic
riders, this time on international duty with the USA.

Little did anyone know that this euphoria would
turn so quickly to deflation for the speedway world,
not for Bruce, after the golden boy won in controversial
circumstances the next World Championship Final in
the massive, iconic Los Angeles Coliseum right on his
own doorstep in California. The whole speedway world
went into shock when, in a carefully scripted move as
it turned out, Bruce announced his retirement from
the sport on the rostrum after he had received the
World Championship trophy in front of 30,000 ecstatic
spectators.

Everyone has his own view of the incident when
Bruce clashed with the top English rider Kenny Carter
in the Coliseum, but even after all these years of
analysis, it would seem that the right decision was

made when Carter was excluded for the incident, and for what it is worth, that is my view. But it was a newspaper man's dream because cool, calm, Californian Penhall and Carter, the highly motivated gritty Yorkshireman, were already deadly enemies. I will not forget the sight of Kenny's dad, Mal, being escorted from the track by two very large LA policeman after his frustrations boiled over at his son's exclusion. And even Ivan Mauger, then Carter's manager, saying things which were over the top in the uproar that followed. Controversy makes headlines for the press and the Penhall/Carter duel ticked all the boxes and received exceptional headlines in most national papers in those days when they did give a hoot what happened in the international sport that was speedway. It made front-page news with a colour photo, of course, in the next week's *MCN*. Fantastic.

Away from the cauldron of California, but in the white heat of an earlier *Motor Cycle News*-sponsored Golden Helmet match race at the Shay, Carter's home track, they had clashed, and in the pits, Penhall showed me the marks where Carter had run over his boot! "Look what he's done!" an irate American said to me, expletive deleted. The rivalry was intense and did not need to be made up, it became obvious when they confronted other each on the track. They did hate one another. They had to beat one another. Second wasn't an option for that pair of champions. As it was for many rugged speedway riders over the years, some fair, some not so fair at all, many times. It was a tough sport, played by tough people sometimes.

Me, right, at Halifax handing the late Kenny Carter
MCN's Golden helmet match race championship with
MCN glamour girl, Zena.

In the American Final, Bruce won on 14 points with
Les Collins second on 13, so close to becoming world
champ like his brother Peter, with Dennis Sigalos third
on 12. Philosophical Les, 25 years later, said to me,
"Don't forget, I was the last rider ever to beat Penhall!"
which was true.

It was quite a night for the press in LA. Stories were
bounding onto the page. Penhall's rostrum retirement,
Brit Les runner-up in the world, and it all took time for
the interviews. I left the stadium to go back to the hotel
at around midnight, mulling over the night's amazing
happenings, but halfway there, I realised here I was
walking in a suburb in downtown LA after midnight

with a camera round my neck, wearing a bright red and yellow *Motor Cycle News* anorak, and on each corner, there were little gangs of people and only then did I realise I was the only white person on the street! Still, I spoke to them all and reached the hotel safely of course.

In the Coliseum, Bruce had his own motives. He thought he had achieved everything he wanted to in the sport – what could be better than back-to-back World Championship wins – the best in the world for two years?

He had his future mapped out to become a Hollywood acting superstar, and the World Final simply became a backdrop for his entry into the mega *CHiPs* TV drama series where he played a motorcycle cop, Bruce Nelson, 1982/83. It will be the first and only time in history that a speedway rider, who won a World final as Bruce did in 1982 was also being filmed at the meeting for a part in a TV series! Absolutely amazing.

That he never quite achieved what he wanted in the world of acting is another story in his life. He was scarred early on by personal tragedies too, with the death of his parents in an air crash and the death many years later of his own son Connor while working on a roadside construction site for his father's company. He was hit by a car driven by someone over the drink-drive limit. As a friend, it was difficult for me to take in and make sense of, but for Bruce as a father and for his wife, words cannot even begin to express the losses the family had to withstand.

Chapter 17

Tragedy off track

Kenny Carter was also a friend of mine and we got on well. It was his own personal tragedy that in 1986 he was to take the life of his wife Pam, then kill himself with the same shotgun, an awful, appalling day for the Carter family from which you'd never recover, and for speedway. It is an understatement to say that speedway was stunned with the terrible, unprecedented news.

I was on a day off when Kenny died, and before the days of mobile phones, remember, I was told that Kenny had rung me in the office that day. It was by then of course too late for me to call back. On Wednesday, 28 May 1986, *MCN* splashed the headline on the front page "Carter deaths: Alan races on." The story said: Plucky Alan Carter raced to tenth place at the West German GP despite the shadow cast by the tragic death of his brother Kenny.

The younger Carter was told in the Nürburgring paddock that his brother and sister-in-law Pam had both been killed in a shooting at Kenny's Yorkshire home.

But Alan decided against returning home until after Sunday's race. "I have a contract to race and that's what I thought it best to do," said a shocked Carter.

"I'm trying to block out everything but road racing at the moment," he said, but who quickly travelled back to Britain on Monday. I did a special tribute to Kenny Carter inside the same issue. That was headlined The Showman, with a strapline of: "Speedway will be a less colourful sport without you Kenny. Rest in peace, ace."

The article asked: "Is there a typical Yorkshireman? Gruff of voice and blunt of nature? One who called a spade a bloody shovel? Kenny Carter was all that – and more. Through ability and sheer hard work, he scaled the heights of a demanding sport where riders' careers are made or broken, in split seconds, rather than hours.

His dedication to success was foremost and he built around himself an aura which few can live up to.

People who do are called superstars. Kenny Carter was a superstar. If you were a friend or enemy, and he had plenty with his forthright approach to sport and life, you couldn't ignore him.

For English speedway, it is a tragedy he did not win the World Championship. He would have made a great ambassador and been thoroughly at home with all the pressures such an exalted position has. The cricket world has been split down the middle for years by another Yorkshireman, Geoffrey Boycott, who left people either for or against him. Kenny could instil in people the same defensive or aggressive postures. The speedway fans and media have been unable to ignore Kenny ever since he burst onto the scene as a precocious teenager with second division Newcastle in 1978. To those who would listen then, he would say he was going to be world champion. No speedway fan will forget the World Final in Los Angeles in 1982 when he crashed in a controversial race with Bruce Penhall when they were both flat out to win the title.

History shows Carter was excluded from the race and Penhall went on to win the championship.

It was the nearest Carter came to winning the sport's major crown.

In 1983 Carter finished a dejected fourth in the World Final, which was unhappily his last.

Injuries side-lined him for the next two finals. He badly broke his leg at Cradley Heath early in 1984 but still managed to win the British championship three months later.

In 1985, the injury jinx struck again in a world round in Sweden. Some riders tend to sit back and say, No one will sponsor me, help!

Not KC! He went out and got his own by sheer hard work – cars, vans, bikes, ancillary equipment, helmets, leathers, he was sponsored for the lot through sheer hard graft.

Even then he had the flair for the big sell. Remember last year's van with the legend on the back door. "You are following the world's most famous motor cycling brothers."

He was a showman of the old school, whose flamboyance was bound to make some enemies. Off the track, he had started to set up a sports consultancy in Halifax, signing up Olympic gold medallist javelin thrower Tessa Sanderson MBE and he was team manager of younger brother Alan in his 250 Grand Prix efforts. Tessa was signed up just two months before the tragedy, and that too was headline news in *MCN* under the banner "Tessa joins Kenny's new spearhead."

If I, as a personal friend of Kenny's for many years, had been asked to write the final scenario of the Carter story, this human tragedy could not even have been hinted at.

It is a tragedy for speedway – in Yorkshire he had been the kingpin for Halifax and Bradford. It is a tragedy for England – at a time when they were trying to re-group their international team. He loved riding for his country, always gave of his best, and was disappointed if his team didn't match up to his highest standards."

Carter and his wife Pamela were found shot dead at their West Yorkshire farmhouse.

Police who were investigating the tragedy said they were not looking for a third person, and there was no one else at the house at the time. Pamela's body was found outside their home at Bradshaw, near Halifax, while Carter was discovered inside the house. The bodies were discovered by a next-door neighbour at their Grey Horse Farm.

Carter himself was a very good road racer and had many a practice spin at Donington Park with younger brother Alan, the Grand Prix rider.

The coroner Mr James Turnbull was told Pam died of shock and haemorrhage due to gunshot wounds, principally to the right lung and heart. Carter suffered gunshot wounds to his left lung.

I will always wonder what Kenny wanted to say to me when he rang me on my day off. I try to remember better days with Kenny, including in 1984, when with a broken leg (broken at Cradley some five weeks earlier), he competed in a British semi-final at Oxford and qualified for the British Final, finishing third in a rain-affected meeting; despite the injury. I knocked on the door of his motorhome in the pits after the meeting and was told to come in. Kenny was in pain but elated (he had to be lifted on and off the bike for each race) and we had a really good chat about his success in overcoming adversity. I was the only journalist who got in to see him that night, I believe. A remarkable young man. In the early 80s, Kenny was as good a rider as anyone in the world. But speedway becomes inconsequential, an irrelevance during such dreadful times.

It had started out all so brightly for one of the most talented riders of his generation. I am sure he would have become world champion if he had kept his cool and taken the right advice on Los Angeles Final night, especially about which tyres he should have used. The whiz kid born in Halifax on 28 March 1961 started off his shale career with National League side Newcastle Diamonds in 1978, the year he also signed for British League outfit Halifax Dukes. In that debut year among the big boys, 16 matches gave him an average of over five points a match. A very good start to his Dukes career. He just got better and better, in 1979 as a precocious kid, he upped that average to over eight points a match, and second overall in the team's season averages.

The following year, Carter upped his average again to nearly nine points per match and again second in the averages. In a remarkable career, Carter was top of Halifax's averages from 1981 up until 1985. In 1981 the average was just over 10 points per match, in 1982 an even greater figure was achieved of an amazing 11.030 per match, keeping his average up to over 10 the following year (1983), dropping slightly to a nine pointer in 1983 before 1985 saw him reach double figures again and an average of 10.133. It takes riding of a very high calibre to achieve these sorts of figures in what then was the toughest league in the world, riding practically every night against most of the top riders in the universe.

Kenny Carter looking at my programme, watched by Peter Collins, UK World team Cup round, Reading, 1983.

On the international stage, Carter rode 55 times for his country after making nine appearances for the up-and-coming riders in the Young England set up. He became British champion twice, winning in 1984 and retaining it the following year, 1985. It was often said that the British League Riders' Championship had a tougher field than any World Final, with each of the British clubs' number ones competing. That was no obstacle to the talented tyke who won that particular championship twice, first winning in 1981 and retaining it in 1982. He struck international gold when he won the world pairs championship for England in

1983 with Peter Collins. Carter scored 15 points and PC 10 to pip the Australians, Billy Sanders and Gary Guglielmi by one point in Ullevi Stadium, Gothenburg, Sweden. He was also a silver medallist twice in that championship in 1982 and 1985. He also had two silver medals riding for England in the world team championship in 1981 and 1983.

Speedway is one of the toughest sports in the world and Carter knew that too. He broke his leg in 1984 and in under a year he broke the same leg in the Intercontinental Final in a wet meeting at Vetlanda, Sweden, which eliminated him from any further competition in the 1985 World Championship. He made just one other World Championship meeting, a semi-final in 1986 before the tragic shooting.

He made just three World Final appearances (remember the World Final was a one-off individual meeting in those days, not a series of finals) with a debut at the last Final ever staged at Wembley Stadium (1981) when he scored 11 points for fifth place behind winner Bruce Penhall, runner-up Ole Olsen and third-placed Tommy Knudsen. Erik Gundersen also scored 11 points but was placed fourth. Some rider, some debut. He won three races that night, had a second place, but in his fourth ride, he retired. Onto Los Angeles for the American staging of one of the most controversial finals ever staged with Carter centre staged in "that" crash with Penhall, which eventually left Carter reeling in fifth place on 10 points.

Again, 12 months on, speedway's World Final had moved onto Norden, a big German track in the middle of nowhere with odds-on favourite Egon Muller from the home country. He was looked upon as being a dead cert for victory with his world long track experience, vital on such a big, flat, fast track. He was unbeaten in five rides and took the accolades of 28,000 spectators, albeit only 2,000 less than had been attracted to the Los Angeles event 12 months earlier. Nearly everyone else struggled, although Billy Sanders rode out of his skin for his 12 points and used all his experience of big Aussie tracks to finish runner-up, while Brit Michael Lee scored 11 points for third, which was also impressive. But they had no answer to the speed of Muller when they met. Carter finished fourth on 10 points. It was not as though the Carter family, with tough-guy father Mal at the head, just had one phenomenal motorcycle racer. Carter's younger brother Alan (B 19 August 1964) was an ace road racer, and his claim to fame was that at the age of 18, he became the youngest ever winner of a Grand Prix race. Alan took a Yamaha TZ250 to victory in the 1983 French GP held at Le Mans. But various problems ensued, and young Alan never hit the number one spot again, never fulfilling his potential. However, in 1985, Alan was seventh in the world championships standings. Car dealer dad Mal was behind the successful Pharoah team of Ron Haslam too.

I seem to recall that on Mal's farm in Yorkshire he had several exotic pets which included, I am sure at one time, a bison.

Chapter 18

MCN Golden Helmet days

One of the episodes which gave me great pleasure was when I was part of MCN's sponsorship of the Golden Helmet match race speedway series which began in 1980 and continued very successfully for a couple of years after that.

Speedway's British match race championhip had been around since the sport started and had many formats. In the 1950s it was famous for the involvement of the foremost rider Jack Paarker. I believe it was run after most official fixtures in those days and he became such a prolific winner, it was known as "Parker's Pension."

But in most recent times, it was decided monthly. In 1974 and 1975 it was sponsored by the Speedway Star, from 1976 until 1979 by Standard Motorists Centres and after that by MCN. There was an actual "golden helmet" which the winning rider got to wear for the official photos, and I believe it was Gerald Smitherman who produced beautifully manufactured MCN Motor Cycle News race jackets for the riders. Quite special they were.

It was the idea of MCN adverting guro Robin Soar, himself a great speedway fan, for MCN to sponsor the season-long series. Match races were held traditionally before league meetings between two nominated riders, the holder and the nominated challenger. There were two races, and if riders won one race each, a deciding third race was held.

Each month at each venue, MCN's name was plastered on the front of the programme as the Motor Cycle News Golden Helmet match races. With inside articles for the fans, score chart for the match races, full page ad for: "The exciting world of speedway every week in Motor Cycle News. Full reports and pictures on all the Motor Cycle News Golden Helmet match races, plus fixtures, results, news and inside stories on speedway. If it happened on two wheels, it's in Motor Cycle News. On sale every Wednesday at your newsagent. The world's number one." Pretty in your face stuff and just what image-conscious MCN wanted. Great publicity.

In the 4 April 1981 King's Lynn v Poole League Cup meeting, the spotlight in the programme was on the Golden Helmet which that night was due to be between Bo Petersen and Michael Lee.

We said that *MCN* was one of speedway's major sponsors and was very pleased to be backing, for the second year running, the most important Speedway Match Race Championship in the world today. We referred of course to the prestige Golden Helmet races.

"Last year saw American Bruce Penhall successfully defend the title he held throughout the winter months, against John Louis by two legs to nil. John Davis was nominated his next challenger and Penhall again retained the "helmet" when the Reading skipper was forced to concede the title through injury after just one leg had been raced. The Dane, Hans Nielsen took the title from Penhall after a deciding leg had been staged.

"Nielsen's reign was short lived, when he was beaten both at Wolverhampton and at King's Lynn by Dave Jessup. Jessup lost the title the following month to Belle Vue's Chris Morton who was finally defeated by another Dane, Bo Petersen. Petersen lost the Belle Vue leg but won the Hackney encounter after their first race ended in a dead heat. Petersen won the decider at Leicester. The racing was terrific and 1981 should be just as exciting."

We gave £400 to the monthly winner and £200 to the loser, "a substantial increase" on last season, we reported.

It captured the imagination of the speedway public, and national papers ran the results of the *MCN* competition, with me sometimes acting as their "stringer" and sending in results to them directly after each challenge.

We used to take the *MCN* beach buggy, normally seen in its red and yellow colours at our international road race meetings and our own glamour girls who used to go among the crowd distributing *MCN* stickers.

For me it was an exciting time. I went to all the match races wherever they were held, presented the Golden Helmet to the winner with a bottle of champagne on the centre green. I never had a company car, *MCN* always paid me mileage, AA rate, for using my own car and, boy oh boy, I put in the mileage for the match races, and it was a "Golden" pay day for me as well as the riders in those far-off days, whether it be Reading, Halifax, Hackney, Wolves, Cradley or Eastbourne.

Mentioning Eastbourne, it was a sensational development at that track which after much thought brought an eventual end to our sponsorship of the Golden Helmet. Michael Lee was due to ride in the match races at Arlington stadium on a Sunday afternoon in June. We all got down there, handed out all our stickers, billed in the programme as the first event.

Only trouble was, no Michael! He never turned up! Speedway's bad boy returned. I don't know, I think he said he'd probably broken down on the M11 or something, but it was amazingly sensational copy for us and all the national papers. We made it onto the back pages of I think the *Sun*, and most of the nationals carried world champ Michael's no-show with our sponsorship name in the articles. Excuse or no excuse, the authorities took swift and retributory action against Lee. He was fined for his non-appearance and stripped of the Golden Helmet even though he won the first leg 24 hours before at King's Lynn. He had lifted the crown, astonishingly for the first time, after three unsuccessful challenges in previous seasons, when as reigning world number one he was winter holder Bo Petersen's first opponent.

Lee equalled the track record at King's Lynn in the opening leg and six days later set up the fastest times of the season at Hackney to wrench the helmet off Petersen's head. Next month Lee brushed aside the challenge of Leicester's Les Collins. He won all four match races and when he inflicted another 2-0 defeat on Kennett at Saddlebow Road, it meant he hadn't lost a single race in his first 10 Golden Helmet encounters. In fact, he will go down in history as the only rider ever to have lost the title without having been beaten in a single race. Lee's helmet ban left the British Speedway Promoters' Association searching for a new champion and they nominated Kennett to face British Champion Steve Bastable for the vacant honour. Each won comfortably enough on their home track but Bastable's hopes dipped when it was announced that the decider would be at one of his least favourite tracks, Wimbledon. His melancholy was understandable, and after leading the Eastbourne skipper for more than three laps, he made a tiny mistake on the last turn and let Kennett through. That first race defeat destroyed his confidence still further and Kennett had no trouble in the second decider.

Surprisingly Bruce Penhall was overlooked as the August challenger, and instead another Englishman Kenny Carter (the fifth successive Brit to be nominated) took up the challenge.

Penhall's non-selection upset Cradley Heath promoter Peter Adams, and at one time it looked as if he might be ruled out of the Golden Helmet for the full season.

Carter survived a collapsed piston in the Halifax legs and then overcame a deep track at Reading that angered the Eastbourne contingent after a neutral venue had been needed to settle the issue.

Referee Alan Todd excluded Kennett for a second bend incident to award the first decider to Carter, who then steamed on to a second victory to collect his first major honour of the season.

The World Final came and went with only one logical opponent for Carter, the World Champion himself. But it was impossible to find suitable September dates for a clash between two Saturday night tracks and eventually everyone agreed to hold back the most exciting set-to of the season until October.

By then the sparks were really flying. Carter had upset both Penhall (and subsequently Cradley fans) by his comments at the Overseas Final regarding Penhall who let other Americans take points off him in a vital race, and then his non-appearance at Dudley Wood for a league match. And the actual challenge lived up to is pre-publicity.

Penhall arrived back from the States far from fully fit and suffering from jet lag and had to give best to Carter in the Midlands leg.

Four days later, Carter was the terrace hero, as the Shay bulged at the seams at the appetising prospect of seeing a Halifax rider retain the championship for the first time.

Penhall made three gates. But after losing the first of the rubber, Carter took note of mentor Ivan Mauger's advice and swept past his American challenger for a 2-1 double.

A delighted Mauger confessed: "I told Kenny where Bruce would try to ride and told Kenny what to do. He carried it out to the letter." It was a clash that provided a fitting finale to a season full of drama and controversy, but the last card had still to be played. *MCN* withdrew their support of the Golden Helmet.

Although the 1982 *Daily Mirror Speedway Yearbook* edited by Peter Oakes reported that: "One can only wonder how much influence Michael Lee's non-appearance at Eastbourne had on that eventual decision."

But *MCN*'s marketing department thought that we'd never get such amazing publicity out of the Golden Helmet again and decided to pull the plug after the season ended. That's the name of the game sometimes, quit when you are ahead.

And I had to go down to Eastbourne the following week for a new *MCN* Golden Helmet challenge, Steve Bastable v Gordon Kennett and me on car mileage once again, from Northamptonshire to Eastbourne and return! Wonderful.

But back to the beginning of *MCN*'s involvement in the Golden Helmet.

We made history in the first year when we had the first dead heat in the competition. For nearly four laps, holder Chris Morton chased after his end-of-season challenger from Hackney and Denmark, Bob Petersen, finally rewarded for season-long consistency that took him to the top of the British League averages.

Coming out of the final bend at Hackney, he made his supreme effort and not even referee John Eglese could separate the front tyres as the pair of them crossed the line together.

Morton was to claim, "I thought that I had won it," but the official declared a dead heat, and perhaps that was the decision that gave Petersen the boost needed to win the next leg, forced a decider at Leicester and went on to inflict a double defeat on a by then battered and bruised Morton, who, the previous week, had sailed straight through the safety fence at Swindon.

So, Petersen opened the 1981 campaign as the reigning *Motor Cycle News* Golden Helmet match race championship.

But the 1980 season started with winter holder Bruce Penhall beating off the challenge of John Louis two races to nil at Ipswich and 2–0 again at Cradley Heath. The first challenger of the season had awful luck. Louis was leading the first leg at Ipswich's Foxhall Heath venue when an electrical fault forced his retirement onto the centre green, it also meant a switch to a slower machine for the second race loss.

The second leg was unfortunate for Louis too. He trapped in front twice, only to stop on both occasions.

The American beat challenger John Davis two races to nil at Reading, and the second leg due at Cradley Heath was a walkover for Penhall, with Davis unfit. Because of conflicting overseas commitments, the match race series was a little disjointed and there was a near two-month gap between one leg and the next.

But Penhall's next challenger was the nominated Hans Nielsen. That clash of the titans went to a third deciding leg. Wolverhampton star Nielsen showed his mastery of his own Monmore Green track when he defeated Penhall 2-0, but predictably Penhall hit back with a 2-0 win at his own Cradley Heath track. At neutral track Birmingham, Nielsen became the new Golden Helmet holder with a 2-0 victory.

Next up challenger was Dave Jessup, who in a supreme peformance defeated Nielsen 2-1 at Wolverhampton and 10 days later became the new Golden Helmet holder with 2-0 race victories before his home King's Lynn fans.

Jessup held the title for only a month and three days, and it was his World Team Cup colleague Chris Morton who took it off him, winning at both Belle Vue and King's Lynn, including two from the back victories that were so typical of the rider who did so much to enliven the 1980 season with his spurts to the front. Morton's next challenger was Petersen, then came the dramatic dead heat, the first in the competition, which gave Petersen the accolade of being the winter holder after a 2-0 defeat of Morton at neutral track Leicester on October 28 on a by then battered and bruised Morton, who, the previous week had sailed straight through the safety fence at Swindon.

We made history in that first year when we had that dead heat at Hackney, not even referee John Eglese could separate the front tyres as the pair of them crossed the line together.

Morton was to claim: "I thought that I had won it," but the official declared a dead heat.

So, Petersen opened the 1981 campaign as the reigning Motor Cycle News Golden Helmet match race championship.

We gave £400 to the monthly winner and £200 to the loser, "a substantial increase" on last season, we reported.

It captured the imagination of the speedway public and national papers ran the results of the MCN competitiion, with me sometimes acting as their "stringer" and sending in results to them directly after each challenge.

We used to take the MCN beach buggy, normally seen in its red and yellow colours at our international road race meetings and our own glamour girls who used to go among the crowd distributing MCN stickers.

For me it was an exciting time. I went to all the match races wherever they were held, presented the Golden Helmet to the winner with a bottle of champagne on the centre green.

Petersen lost his opening defence of the Golden Helmet to reigning world champion Michael Lee, losing 2–0 at King's Lynn and Hackney. Leicester's Les Collins was nominated but lost to Lee, also 2–0 at home and away.

It was fellow England international Gordon Kennett who was next nominated. Lee beat Kennett at King's Lynn on a Saturday night 2–0 and the second leg was to take place 24 hours later at Kennett's home track at Eastbourne. We all travelled down to Eastbourne's Arlington stadium on a lovely June day. We handed out all our stickers to the expectant crowd before the first event. Only trouble was, no Michael! He never turned up! Speedway's bad boy returned. I don't know, I think he said he'd probably broken down on the M11 or something, but it was amazingly sensational copy for us and all the other national papers. We made it onto the back pages of I think the Sun, and most of the nationals carried world champ Michael's no-show with our sponsorship name in the articles. Excuse or no excuse, the authorities took swift and retributory action against Lee. He was fined for his non-appearance and stripped of the Golden Helmet even though he'd won the first leg 24 hours before at King's Lynn.

Lee's helmet ban left the British Speedway Promoters' Assocation searching for a new challenger and they nominated British champion Steve Bastable for the vacant honour. Each won comfortably enough on their own track but Bastable's hoped dipped when it was announced that the decider would be at one of his least favourite tracks, Wimbledon. His melancholy was understandable, and after leading the Eastbourne skipper for more than three laps, he made a tiny mistake on the last turn and let Kennett through. That first race feat destroyed his confidence still further and Kennett had to trouble in the second decider.

Surprisingly Bruce Penhall was overlooked as the August challenger, and instead another Englishman Kenny Carter (the fifth successive Brit to be nominated) took up the challenge.

Penhall's non selection upset Cradley Heath promoter Peter Adams, and at one time it looked as if he might be ruled out of the Golden Helmet for the full season.

Carter survived a collapsed piston in one of the Halifax legs and then overcame a deep track at Reading that angered the Eastbourne contingent after a neutral venue had been needed to settle the issue. Referee Alan Todd excluded Kennett for a second bend incident to award the first decider to Carter, who then steamed on to a second victory to collect his first major honour of the season.

The world final came and went with only one logical opponent for Carter, the world champion himself. But it was impossible to find suitable September dates for a clash between the two Saturday night tracks and eventually everyone agreed to hold back the most exciting set-to of the season until October.

Penhall arrived back from the States far from fully fit and suffering from jet lag and had to give best to Carter in the Midlands leg.

Four days later, Carter was the terrace hero, as The Shay bulged at the seams as the appetising prospect of seeing a Halifax rider retain the championhip for the first time.

Penhall made three gates. But after losing the first of the rubber, Carter took note of mentor Ivan Mauger's advice and swept past his American challenger for a 2–1 double.

A delighted Mauger confessed: "I told Kenny where Bruce would try to ride and told Kenny what to do. He carried it out to the letter." It was a clash that provided a fitting finale to a season full of drama and controversy. But the last card had still to be played. MCN withdrew their support of the Golden Helmet.

Although the 1982 Daily Mirror Speedway Yearbook edited by Peter Oakes reported that: "One can only wonder how much influence Michael Lee's non-appearance at Eastbourne had on that eventual decision."

But MCN's marketing department thought that we'd never get such amazing publicity out of the Golden

Helmet again and decided to pull the plug after the season ended. That's the name of the game sometimes, quit while you are ahead.

There was plenty of cracking racing for the MCN Golden Helmet. All riders gave stellar performances, and I believe we enhanced all of the venues that staged our sponsored match race championships with our presence, putting on a grand show for the fans, a big extra for thousands of fans to watch and get involved with.

Chapter 19

MCN state of our sport!

MCN loved campaigns, and on 17 December 1980, I organised a three-page feature entitled "The state of our sport." The headline shrieked, "Let's hit the space age!" – and "Speedway must present a better show if it wants to keep the paying public happy."

I'm afraid I still think the same 40 years later. Without a proper show, speedway is in trouble. It must give value for money. One of the poorest decisions was to axe the old second-half races, made on grounds of not having to pay riders for extra rides was a big mistake. But how jet-setting riders would take to this again now when all they have to think after any meeting, they have been in is to quickly jet to the next country to race again the next day. Gone are the days, unfortunately, when riders often mingled with supporters after a meeting in the stadium bars! But I do understand that times change, but some, not for the better.

That is the nature of the beast. To make a living, speedway riders, unlike pampered footballers, have to crisscross the globe to ride in Poland, Sweden, Denmark, Germany, Australia for some, to make a living. This is done for all the summer months, week in, week out. So, the traditional second half for star riders, wearing out their expensive engines in "extra" races after a league match, might not be to their liking.

Why not then replace the old second half with other attractions for the spectators who up to that time have seen, let's face it, only some actual 15 minutes of racing, spread over an hour and a half show.

Could not junior racing be employed to give our up-and-coming stars of tomorrow great track time, which is the only way to becoming a successful rider. Augmented by a sidecar league, with the spectacular Aussie style outfits, representing the club itself. I helped to increase their popularity later in my life in the UK and they are great value for money, very spectacular. They would get the spectators' adrenalin pumping.

Australia and America have always had excellent mixed events with speedway involved. Speedway riders from kiddies on tiny bikes up to adults. Why not the UK. The thriving dirt track riders put on a great show with enthusiastic riders hurling anything round speedway style tracks on huge Harleys, Indians, Triumphs and BSAs. They could be incorporated into a speedway show. Anything for great variety. Anything is worth a try to give the spectators more – and speedway needs to attract a new breed of spectator, because as is well known, the "old" guard of speedway supporter, people like me, have either got too old to go to regular speedway meetings or have lost interest over the years because of what they regard as a poorer show placed before them week after week.

Youngsters' involvement in the sport is essential, on track and on the terraces. Otherwise, it can only be stagnation.

In my survey in 1980, British champion Eric Boocock said:

"Basically, we in charge of speedway are not putting on a good show. The rule book is too big. I think we should have about eight pages on how to run a meeting." I believe that is also true today, re-write the rule book to make it easier for promoters to make up their teams and not have to rely on putting one rider before another because of a 0.1 difference in riders averages.

With Poland flexing their muscle as the world's leading nation and not allowing top riders to ride in more than one league is an abuse of power. But the UK is fighting back and has for several years been trying to concentrate on bringing young riders on. That is the way forward. Find your own stars, they will rise to the surface given the right amount of track time. It's what happened in the 1960s when the Provincial League found its own stars. The same will happen again. Youngsters must and are being given every chance to shine.

We were the world's leading nation in the 1970s, now we are behind countries like Denmark and

Sweden in terms of interest in domestic league content. To Poland I say, everyone has their day in the sun, and although it seems unlikely there will be much of a change in Polish superiority, I am sure one will come, I don't know how or why, but it will happen. Something will happen to knock them off their perch. That is simply how life works. But then along came a worldwide pandemic, and speedway had big problems along with many more sports.

My own gripes were that presentation at meetings was appalling. I held up Wimbledon as a shining example of how a track should run a slick show. "Track staff are turned out in colourful attire and smartly walk out to do their duties. On other tracks, staff changing into overalls on the centre green is quite common. What a way to start a show! Incidentally, Wimbledon track staff wore *MCN* anoraks for a time, which were the same colours as the Dons, red and yellow.

"Speedway is fast and exciting to watch, but it must be run quickfire. Interminable delays between races with broken down old tractors unable to grade the track and seized up starting gates should except for the direst of circumstances be a thing of the past, but they aren't.

"If you lose continuity in a match, you lose half its appeal. Speedway's beauty is that everything happens before the public's eyes. It's all laid out for the fans, unlike road racing where riders disappear from sight each lap and the whole race can be decided out of view. Speedway has no such problems."

That is still true today, I believe. I also went on to say an end to guest riders should be included in any long-term plans for speedway. And that has never been addressed. I also asked in the interests of British speedway that there should be a National Training Programme established. "To keep our place on top of the international stage we need a proper training programme under one specialist to keep an eye on the talented youngsters." Such a scheme has now been implemented for several years, and we will reap the benefits long term. I did herald the advent of the British Youth Championship, which is a terrific addition for young riders trying to break into the sport. Its meetings, for all age groups on 125, 250 and 500cc bikes riders are simply superb and must continue to get more young riders back in the sport. They have helped put many riders on the way to track success, and many more will be helped and unveiled if they are given a fair chance and plenty of track time in such meetings and in regular team appearances. Maybe the 15-year-olds on 500s could be an essential part of a speedway night out, either before the meeting or directly after a league match which would entertain the public, give them more races, more value for money and valuable track time for the youngsters trying to break into the sport.

Peter Collins, then recently retired from the sport had a big grouse about dangerous tracks in the country, saying that at least 70 per cent of them "are very dangerous."

"With our bikes going even quicker than ever before, safety fences and track widths should be examined. With faster bikes you need more room. Straight and bend width need to be of the FIM minimum laid down standard, and in England a lot of them are not."

Luckily, a lot of criticism of dangerous track fences has been addressed with the introduction of the air fences to the sport's tracks, which although far from perfect, have helped many riders avoid serious injury. PC's favourite tracks had wooden style fencing, as at his own Belle Vue Hyde Road track, "as you can bounce back," whereas with the wire fence system it is what is behind them that is the problem, "with the girders, posts, track lighting standards that the wire is hung on." But as I said, most of these problems have been eradicated with air fences inside the traditional wire, wood or concrete "fences" which has saved speedway.

The speed of modern-day bikes is a worry. Tracks in Britain have not kept pace with safety as some other nations have done. Mainly because tracks are still in use in very old stadiums. Is the answer to reduce the power of bikes? It's been tried before but has always failed, riders and engine builders always build faster engines. Rev limiters look like one way to go to reduce power. Maybe we should have stage one tuned bikes for youngsters, stage two bikes for intermediates and stage three for the experts. In motor racing, they don't give the most powerful racing Formula One car to a 16-year-old to drive, but speedway kind of does.

And finally, I would love to see half a dozen or more tracks laid out on the lines of the new Leicester speedway stadium. Mainly because speedway tracks inside the old greyhound stadiums, which was how speedway was introduced to the UK in 1928, are going to be a thing of the past.

Chapter 20

The press corps, Simon Wigg

One year as a member of the world's press corps, I got to sit in a palatial stadium in glamorous California for a World Final, as in Los Angeles Coliseum in 1982. The next year we had to walk over a grass field in a country stadium in the middle of nowhere to report from Norden in Germany for the next! As did the crowd who attended of course. It was a big culture shock to everyone, supporters and press alike.

During practice, it became absolutely certain that the huge track, almost built on long track dimensions, that the rider on the fastest machine, and the one who could handle it expertly and with precision, would be the winner.

Egon Muller was perhaps the strangest winner of all world titles, a German club entertainer/singer, who for part of his act dressed as a woman! But boy oh boy could Egon ride a racing motorcycle fast, and as it turned out at Norden much faster than anyone else on the shale too.

Egon Muller was an extraordinary performer on the long track scene, which was massive in Germany and on his day was practically unbeatable. He was an extrovert and a huge star in his homeland. In Germany for that one-off World Final, he was unbeatable too, winning with a 15-point maximum. Though Egon did little in Britain, riding only a handful of matches for Coatbridge (1973) and Hull (1976), on the continent he was a superstar and a spectacular rider, whose endeavours, especially on his beloved German long tracks, were legendary.

At an appearance at the international Ace of Aces, the biggest grass track in the world in 1990, organised by top promoter Ian Barclay (backed all the way by his redoubtable wife Christine), plus Dickie Staff and Grubby Sharp, Muller was late.

The story goes that Muller was detained for a chat for a while by customs men at Heathrow. He was going to be far too late being driven in a van from the airport to the Hampshire venue. A plan was hatched for the helicopter taking fans for a jolly five-minute ride round at the Aces field to look for Muller in the van and found it on the M4. The van landed in a field next to the motorway; Muller, helmet and his own handlebars in hand, leapt out of the van and climbed over a fence to get a helicopter ride straight into the Aces track!

Barclay ran the best grass track events in the UK, bar none. His memory lived on for me after the demise of the Ace of Aces, as Ian was a "star" of one of my favourite TV programmes, the BBC series Time Team, where Ian was for many series, the expert digger-driver who opened up the trenches for the archaeologists to dive into to find the gold and the skeletons of old. As Sir Tony Robinson's Time Team is still repeated endlessly on TV, I still occasionally catch glimpses of Ian on his digger, which brings back happy memories for me.

Playing the goat, expecting a wet grass track meeting
October 1993, information from Mum's handwriting
on back of photo.

One of Muller's greatest rivals on the world long tracks for many years was Simon Wigg, who became my best friend in speedway for many years, and his early death was a personal tragedy, as it was to his family and the whole speedway world.

Wiggy was an extrovert, showman and great rider, who took professionalism in the sport to new heights. He enjoyed a good laugh, and we talked on the phone for hours at a time, airing his lucid views of speedway, grass track, long track. And I was getting paid for this too and many good stories emanated from Simon this way!

I listened to the master as stories kept pouring out of him, many being printed in *MCN*. He was track racing through and through, devoted to putting on a good show everywhere he went on his immaculate stable of machines. He was another rider who had *MCN* at heart and he would do anything for us if possible. We got his "lightened" long track bike in a sauna once for a photo shoot opportunity. Sauna, lose weight? A little tenuous no doubt, but a good idea at the time, we thought. You lose weight in a sauna and Wiggy's bike had been trimmed of a few pounds too...

Wiggy was passionate about his sport and had brilliant ideas of how a meeting should be run for the entertainment of the crowd, with pumping rock music between races and other innovations he'd seen at the long tracks in Germany which became "events" not to be missed by anyone in the locality. And of course,

Wiggy was a hero to many of the long track fans in Europe through his fearless riding and success at the biggest meetings, week in and week out throughout his illustrious career.

At home with the late great Simon Wigg acting up for the camera. Top professional. My camera.

He was certainly a darling of the crowds wherever he went, and on the rostrums in Germany was able to talk to the adoring fans in their own language.

Days and nights with Wiggy at World Long Track Finals were never dull. He had a Dutch racing licence at the time during one disagreement with UK racing authority but went nuts when they played the Dutch national anthem and not "God Save the Queen" when he was on the rostrum!

After one of his world long track wins, *Speedway Star* editor Richard Clark and I were in the shower room directly after his success, interviewing him although he was stark naked in the showers. Even when he was asked to fill the obligatory bottle with urine for the drugs test, he did not stop talking – through a half-closed door this time.

Simon was an early convert to sports psychology, diet and exercise. Slavi Petkovsky, who grew up in Denmark was the name of the guy Simon used. On the occasion we met up with Slavi, Simon had suffered a very deep gash to his leg after his throttle stuck open in a German grass track and he got tangled up as the bike kept going end over end. Wigg's leathers were ripped, and he thought he'd broken his leg, but a large area of his left calf had been worn away, parts of the injury were black from the spinning tyre. He was told the wound would take months to heal, and he thought his season over. It was then that Simon contacted Slavi.

I stood by as Slavi, in his operating theatre, injected sterilised water into Simon's muscle. The photo we used as the treatment was being done showed Simon in considerable pain and it was not for the camera; it was genuine, it hurt. Simon said: "It felt like an explosion going off in your leg. I would rather crash 100 times than have the treatment. It was terrible but it worked." The treatment Slavi claimed opened the muscles and got the circulation going again. Acupuncture or massage takes about 12 hours for results, his treatment took three minutes. "I also did have intense electro-therapy, some acupuncture, vacuum treatment and ultra-violet ray treatment. It turned me into a winner again," added a relieved Simon.

He went on to win the world long track title in 1993, his fourth world title. Hearing the screams from Wiggy, I thought I had ventured a little too near the action that day!

Slavi had what I thought was a severe exercise regime which would have made most athletes throw up, but Simon kept going right to the end without much of a murmur. The Yugoslav-born fitness expert was called "Madman or Genius?" in Denmark. It was easy to see why as some of his bizarre techniques had included one of his subjects performing press ups above a sharp foot-long wooden stake, hitting people in the chest with a baseball bat in a frosty Danish forest, and taping up sportsman's eyes and mouths before starting exercise, apparently. Simon didn't go that far.

But Simon himself was a publicity man's dream. Ask him to do anything for the camera and he'd happily oblige. A feature at his Berkshire country home had him riding his sit-on mower, cutting the grass, then riding his Harley while wearing the German Golden Helmet championship trophy, and later on, leaping off the handlebars of his long track bike so we could get a picture of him in mid-air! All in his famous green racing Kevlar's, backed up by his huge green Iveco motorhome.

But a visit to his workshops showed the true professionalism of the man. You could eat your dinner off the floor, it was so clean. And there they were, rows of speedway, grass track and long track bikes, all prepared and honed to perfection by mechanics Brett Walton and Mick Trevett, so that Simon could be at his best for his next action, be it in England, Germany, Eastern Europe or throughout trips to deepest Russia riding his racing motorcycles for a living.

Simon would do anything for publicity and *MCN*, but one of my ideas in 1987 nearly ended up with a damaged rider! I had a notion of a feature to find out how fast in a straight line one of his Godden speedway bikes would go flat out, as it had never been done before in this way on a standard bike with no aerodynamic fairings added for airflow.

Simon accepted and we went to Bruntingthorpe airfield, Leicestershire, where *MCN* did top speed tests on road bikes too, and BBC TV *Top Gear* too.

But this was on tarmac, not grass or shale.

We set up the timing equipment and Simon warmed up the bike for his first attempt. Simon was doing well over 100mph when he tried to stop and slammed shut the throttle. What happened next became a blur. The bike went into the biggest, most horrible tank slapper you have ever seen. It was a blessing that Simon was one of the best riders in the world, and his quick thinking took him onto the grass at the side of the track and he wrestled it to a standstill without falling off! He said it was the biggest tank slapper he'd ever had in his racing career. I went white and could see the headlines if it had all gone wrong: "*MCN* seriously injure world champion long tracker Simon Wigg in track test."

But, undeterred, Simon got back on and learned to roll off the throttle much more gently after top speed had been achieved, which meant no more tank slappers, thank goodness. He was even more of a star that day.

As nobody had, as far as I know, ever done top speed runs of a speedway bike on tarmac, we were having to make it up as we went along before Simon could make an attempt. Over to his brother Julian, who made some essential modifications to the brake-less methanol burning Godden. Julian added extra trail to the forks for stability in a straight line and fitted an engine kill switch on the left handlebar. In speedway to cut the engine, you pull your right hand off the bars, but of course, at such speeds, Julian did not want his brother to do that at Bruntingthorpe.

The knobbly rear speedway tyre, not safe for high speeds on tarmac, was replaced by a 19-inch Pirelli Phantom front road tyre by Julian. The possibility of stopping after high-speed runs was a big topic. Don Godden had once tried a Lockheed rear calliper and disc in grass track and Julian fitted one such item to Simon's mount.

But other than that, it was a standard speedway bike that would have been used in league racing on 350-yard shale ovals. With a 52-tooth sprocket giving a 6.8:1 final drive ratio, Wigg was ready, if nervous for his first runs. Of course, the bike had no gearbox with its enormous torque pulling it through to 9000 revs. With 104mph predicted by Julian, Simon was off. Simon said he did not need the brakes as the 14:1 compression stopped the bike on its own when the throttle was gently rolled off, it was able to stop in under 200 yards. Julian's work had not been needed. He was not amused.

But it took some wrestling as the bars wanted to go all over the place, reported Simon, who had to take off his loose-fitting sponsors' bib because it was billowing out and making control even more perilous as it swished behind him. The bike was hitting 9000 revs very early, so it was decided to fit the tallest and smallest sprocket they had, a 39-tooth Fantic trial bike acquired that morning.

It was almost the size of his old cycle speedway sprocket Simon said. So, Simon prepared a run on a distinctly non-speedway 5.11:1 final drive ratio. A nasty wobble set in at 116mph, which was incredible, but Simon said the wobble had been caused by a side wind because he had to lean into the wind and move the bars to keep it in a straight line.

That might have been enough for most riders, but back on the runway running a 46th tooth sprocket,

5.89:1 ratio in an effort to get the motor to rev out, the bike ran straight and true. Simon's efforts came to an end when a smoke-belching DAF truck charged flat out across our strip...

But the enforced break to calm everyone really fired up our Simon. Another sprocket swop, back to the Fantic 39-toother gave him a scintillating 126mph, then an amazing 127mph pass. Simon tried all sorts of styles, both legs flat out at the back of the bike, left leg only trailing, with his left hand gripping the forks. As *MCN* reported, it takes a certain level of rider commitment to achieve such a spectacular feat of daring. A speed never achieved and recorded properly on a standard 500cc four-stroke single speedway machine and the motor, said Simon, was still 800 revs off the 9000-rev limit, so they reckoned they could top 130mph! Technical help for the feature was given to me by *MCN* road test reporter Tim Thompson.

"Wigg the Thunderer". That's the style it takes to ride at 127mph on tarmac on a standard 500cc speedway engined bike.

Simon gave all *MCN* readers a taste of what it was like to live the life of a professional world-class racer in a page feature we dreamed up in 1994. We followed Simon through 12 days of racing, which took in 3,400 miles in his van to race in four different meetings. I wrote: "A gruelling 3400-mile grand tour of seven countries would be most people's idea of hell, but it's just another day or two at the office for world long track champion Simon Wigg. This typical jaunt took in France, Luxembourg, Belgium, Germany, the Czech Republic, Austria and Hungary." The trip, Wigg told *MCN* readers, began on a Monday when his mechanic Brett Walton and friend Nick Capper loaded up his seven-litre diesel Ford Econoline van with five factory Jawa machines, three speedway bikes and two long trackers on another Wigg's Continental Tours.

First day was a ferry ride, Ramsgate to Dunkirk, for a long track meeting in Altrip, Germany. 500 miles later they stopped at a hotel at 7pm. Next day practice at long track started at 8am. The track record had stood for 13 years, but Wigg broke it. And the meeting was watched by 10,000 people.

The following day saw the intrepid travellers do another 200 miles in the van. Second meeting was a floodlit long track at Vechta, and Wigg finished second to Karl Maier. 70 miles in the van. A day was spent cleaning bikes before they hit the road again for the Czech Republic and the van clocked up another 500 miles, with roads deteriorating badly. A day off was spent shopping in Prague. This time the racing was in a Czech league match with Wigg riding for Pilsen, against Pardubice. He's on his way to a 15-point maximum but, in a rare mistake, lets one rider through because he thinks it's a teammate, but it's an opposition man. Next visit is to Vienna in Austria, 400 miles away.

Bikes were worked on in Vienna before they set off for Miskolc, Hungary for the Continental Speedway semi-final and another 400 miles are clocked up in six hours. Wigg picked up £125 FIM travel money, enough just to pay the hotel bill. Then the slog back home begins, a remarkable 1300 miles, via Vienna, which takes 26 hours.

Wigg arrives home at 4.30pm, 13 days after setting off for the road trip, when he discovered that girlfriend Charlie had been rushed to Milton Keynes hospital in labour. "I got there just in time to witness the birth of our first child, Abigail, at 12.30am the following morning. I eventually got to bed at 4.30am, feeling very tired, but a proud dad!"

MCN readers were as amazed as I was of such an experience from a professional racer plying his trade!

Chapter 21

F1!

In 1982, *MCN* managed to procure a drive in a Formula One car for Bruce Penhall, then the world champion after his sensational riding in the last Final at Wembley in 1981.

The famous March team whose former drivers included Jo Siffert, Niki Lauda and Ronnie Peterson, made available a current F1 car at Silverstone, full pit crew, the works, for Bruce to have a drive of a lifetime in a current state-of-the-art projectile.

It was a great feeling for me, then an avid follower of Formula 1 (and having been to my first British GP staged at Aintree, yes Grand National Aintree, in 1961), to be in the pits as the car was warmed up. What a cracking noise from the car with sponsorship plastered on it from Rothmans and *Newsweek*! Bruce listened to all the advice the March technical team and mechanics on hand gave him in a careful brief before he went out on track. He was dressed this time not in Kevlar "leathers" but an appropriate racing suit and boots. "I'm a little nervous," admitted Bruce, "I don't want to crash millions of pounds worth of car!"

They insisted that whatever they told him, he would stall the car as he set off from pit lane first time round. And Bruce did! But after that he quickly came to grips with the strange transition from sliding a two-wheel speedway bike to using the power of a Formula One engine round the iconic Silverstone track in Northamptonshire, the home of British GP.

He didn't hang around, his times were respectable, we were told, as he got used to the track, never spun it, got the expensive machine back in one piece without a bent wheel or panel and was elated at the brilliant chance *MCN* had afforded him, which is not given to many outside the heady world of four wheels! And all of it featured in an *MCN* exclusive as another off-the-wall adventure!

Yes, we did it. *MCN*'s name got world champion Bruce
Penhall a drive in a March Formula One car at Silverstone,
home of the British Grand Prix. What a day that was for
Bruce and I. Up close with an F1 car, never forget it.

My own four-wheel adventures took me to the
Macau GP in 1990 reporting for *MCN*. Macau is a
region on the south coast of China and reached, when
I went, by a hydrofoil jet boat from Hong Kong about
65 kilometres away, which was exhilarating and the
fastest I ever want to go on water! Macau has the

famous 3.8-mile street circuit with 170mph straights lined with concrete walls. You had to say it made the Isle of Man TT circuit look safe indeed. It's still the only circuit which has races for both cars and motorcycles over the same weekend. That year, I saw the F3 race with Michael Schumacher beating Mika Hakkinen for the win. What a treat. And in the bikes, Steve Hislop won on his Honda RC30, another great performance. After racing, we went into mainland China for a sightseeing day and my roommate for the trip, legendary rider Joey Dunlop sat in the coach smoking, refusing to get out to eat in the designated Chinese restaurant! Joey did like to go to Macau's famous gambling casinos though.

The Macau trip was almost a journalists' holiday for the scribes while reporting on the racing.

The only photo I can find of me on my
one-day tour in China.

My Macau road race press pass, the only full course
one I ever had in my career

Another exotic trip was to Monaco, paid for by the
Italian bike manufacturer Piaggio for the launch of a
moped in the early 80s. The party of non-bike
journalists included the editor of *Reveille*, I believe.
Reveille was a weekly tabloid with exotic photos of
girls, is my best description. We stayed at one of the
best five-star hotels in Monte Carlo, pity there was no
Grand Prix on though, but I had the best meal I ever

had in the Loews Hotel, named after the circuit hairpin outside, best show I've ever seen on stage, where a donkey or some such animal disappeared in a magic act before our eyes. Magic. And I got to have a walk around the famous Monte Carlo casino too, not venturing to put a bet on.

The trip started amazingly as I was one of the few journalists on the trip who hitched a lift on a tiny Bell helicopter, you know, the one with a glass bubble cockpit, from Nice down the coast to Monte Carlo! Absolutely amazing views. Talk about flight of a lifetime. For me anyway. Ironically, the moped was never sold in Britain! And I can't remember ever riding the bike, but perhaps we did.

Top speed figures are a big draw for bike fans. We had top road racer and TT legend Mick Grant regularly do our racer tests at Snetterton. At one test, Mick was screaming round on somebody else's racer which we were testing, but we couldn't get the timing equipment to work, so he was wasting his time riding round at ten tenths to get a top speed.

But we couldn't get him to stop. It is difficult to see someone waving to you to come in doing 130–140mph, so it was off with my anorak to wave at him at the side of the track to make Mick stop. But perhaps Mick just didn't want to stop anyway! He was just having fun on someone else's bike for a start! The pesky antique timing lights which had to be set up on little stands on each side of the track were always trouble and were, I think, very low technology. It was difficult to set up the beam across the track for the bike to break. I remember one road bike test at Bruntingthorpe where we had managed to get the timing lights set ready for a run when out of the distance, someone testing a fast saloon car at full speed ran over one of our tiny lights stands, wrecking it! Probably some idiot from *Top Gear*, I reckon on purpose, in my opinion. No names.

Chapter 22
The TT

I had many other reporting duties at *MCN*, which in the 1970s and 80s was the world's largest selling motorcycle newspaper. It was published weekly, and although it was a national paper, its editorial offices were not, as was traditional, in London but in provincial Kettering, Northants. It was part of the mega EMAP group which had hundreds of leisure titles, but its flagship was always *MCN*. It was its cash-cow. The advertising revenue was immense and if you wanted to buy or sell a bike, your first port of call was the *MCN* small ads.

The biggest single event of the year for *MCN* was the annual Isle of Man TT races. Reporting on them was organised like a military manoeuvre, with chief reporter Norrie Whyte at the helm of the ship! Dozens of hotel bookings were made at the "Mona" hotel, dozens of flights sorted out and reporters were told which race they had to report on and who was to help as and when. Before digital cameras, 35mm film was the norm and the negatives had to be put on planes to be processed in Kettering, not digitised over the internet, so duties sometimes included driving to an airport to pick up the packages and bring them to the office.

At one stay at the Castle Mona, the ace comedian Ken Dodd, who had just done a show on the island, came into the bar late in the evening. The tousled haired joker with the famous buck teeth asked drinkers their names, saying he collected unusual monikers, and started to tell jokes. He couldn't stop himself and he had the room roaring with laughter that night. He performed for hours and it was one of the funniest nights I can remember. Good one, Ken. We got to see his show for nothing.

I was not one of the "elite" road race reporters, with the paper quite rightly prioritising the tarmac sport as that was the main sales winner for *MCN*. I did go several times to the TT with *MCN* but only as a fill in, reserve, feature man. Even the simple "go and interview so and so now, will you" was sometimes difficult to carry out. To find where they were staying on the island, particularly the ordinary rider as opposed to the stars, could pose problems for me. When you found his digs, invariably he was not there, and you had to return with your deadline quickly being eaten away.

In 1979, the unpredictable Manx weather had hit the island yet again, causing many cancellations of races, and the main race was held over to the Monday, which messed up all Norrie's meticulous travel plans. Everyone had to return on their booked flights, but Norrie was to report on the big race, and I was to help too as his "gofer", sitting in the press section of the start and finish grandstand. I felt like royalty. Until the report of a death in the race came to the press box.

Norrie and I had no flights to get off the island and we had to get back to the office as quickly as possible after the race. Big Norrie, well over six foot, who was known to everyone in the world of road racing, engineered a lift for us aboard a small private plane with Alex George, incidentally the winner of the race, and like Norrie, a Scotsman. Alex was on his way to Assen, Netherlands, I think, after winning the F1 and Classic TTs, but the pilot made a brief stop off on the way to Donington airport and Norrie and I grabbed a lift back to the Kettering office, not too far away.

On that flight Alex, who may have been paid in cash for his win, opened his suitcase, and I don't know how much was in there, but I have never seen so much money in my life, before or since.

I went to the island, the mecca for all road race fans, as a youngster, many years before joining *MCN* and it was interesting seeing the island from another perspective as a journalist.

My first trips were much more mundane but were some of the greatest holidays I'd had up to then. For several years I used to take my fortnight's holiday on the island, taking in practice week and race week.

With not much money, it was simple digs for me and my mates. The island was a magical place for motorcycle fans. Even walking down the promenade in Douglas was a history lesson, looking at bikes which had been ridden to the island from all over the world.

There was much raucous behaviour, much drinking, much fun, but never any serious trouble that I witnessed.

Some years we had no transport and just got about the island as best we could. However, one year my friend John Vallender and I decided to hire some wheels. Two wheels. The only thing we could hire for the TT week was, believe it or not, a SCOOTER! It must have been the only scooter on the island and was really embarrassing, but we just got on with it. It was not a new one, and it was usual to push it to make it go, kick-starting it didn't seem to do much. One day just before road closure on the course, with me riding it and John on the pillion, we drove down part of the course with the fans already assembled in their thousands for the next race. We got cheers or jeers from just about everyone, but it was a good laugh! Luckily for us it had: "Hired scooter from Tiger Tim" on the side and I pointed at this sign so that the bike fans could see that I didn't in fact own it but had only hired it! It must have been a rare sight. Me at 5ft 7in riding it with my passenger John towering above me behind at 6ft-something.

We learnt the ropes of where to stay and where best to watch from on the amazing 37-and three-quarter-mile road racecourse. First job after arriving on the island was to get to the Creg-ny-Baa hotel as soon as possible to book a balcony seat for one of the main races. What a view that was, watching the bikes howling down from Kate's Cottage on full chat before breaking fiercely and turning, right in front of your eyes and accelerating off again. Bike racing heaven.

In those days, early morning practice was just that. Very early. We didn't want to miss anything, so at some ungodly hour in the morning around six am, John and I would trudge our way on foot through the streets of Douglas to make for the grandstand to watch. One driver took pity on us though and took us to the racetrack. "Get in, lads, I know where you're going," he said simply.

It was all so magical and laid back. I took a photo of TT hero Giacomo Agostini in the pits, in his immaculate black leathers, with him not three feet away. Ah, those were indeed glory days. No cordons, with star names just a tiny speck on the horizon. Keeping safe, you could get up close to your heroes. I still have the fading colour photo somewhere.

John and I were both pipe smokers and found something called Isle of Man shag tobacco in a Douglas tobacconist. We bought it because of the rude name, I guess. It was "plug" tobacco that had to be rolled up, and I took a few puffs of the evil-smelling stuff and said it was far too strong a smoke for me. But John, who did not like to be beaten, said, no, it was lovely and puffed out clouds of smoke. I have never actually seen someone turn green before, but I swear John did that day as he tried to smoke the island's "revenge" for pipe smokers, the infamous Isle of Man shag tobacco. I bet they don't still make it. I don't want any anyway,

I gave up smoking many, many years ago, thank goodness.

The years I went to the island, Agostini was king on his immaculate MV 350 and 500s. His opposition was mainly the single-cylinder British bikes, which, although good, were nowhere near as fast as the Italian multis. Unfortunately, the glorious Mike Hailwood island era had just finished by the time I got to go to the island as a fan.

The only time I got to see Hailwood, my hero, on his fabulous Honda 250 six-cylinder machine was at a race at Mallory Park for the Race of the Year, and I will never forget the marvellous raucous sound coming out of those six megaphones as he exited Gerard's Bend, with all of those six cylinders eventually all chiming in. Wow. What a sound. The most charismatic racing machine ever in my opinion. Amazing. Years later my friend George Beale built a rare, immaculate replica six-cylinder based in every detail on this precision Japanese machinery, and I was pleased to hear that machine being warmed up and paraded at a Donington Park classic meeting. What memories it evoked. And to meet up again with George was great.

But the TT had a dark side. The unique road course through towns and villages, tree-lined and stone wall-lined for a lot of its distance, killed many riders. With speeds increasing all the time, it was in the end stripped of its World Championship status, which meant only those riders who wanted to go had to go and among those that didn't go included Agostini in the end. But having gone to spectate many times, it is easy to see why people want the ultimate thrill of road racing on the island. It is unique. I am sure it is like a drug, once you have experienced it, you want to continue with the thrill-making.

Everyone, fans included, was always very upset when riders died, and one memory comes flooding back to me. In 1970 a young Spanish rider, Santiago Herrero, went to the island on a fabulously quick 250 Ossa. But he crashed in the Lightweight race. Later in a Douglas pub, me and some others got talking to a young lady who had come in very upset. She was a nurse at Noble's hospital and told us that Herrero had just died. Awfully sad.

My only race-reporting duties, as opposed to island feature writing and helping Norrie Whyte, was a chance one year to be the *MCN* scribe at the Southern 100 road races, which on its smaller course was even more frightening to me than the TT. I stood to one side of the grid during one race as the riders started and ended up jumping back into a deep ditch, they came so close to me. I only made that mistake once.

Riders, if they did not make a bend, rode through the gate into a field, if the farmer had remembered to leave it open for the race. Memories of the meeting are vague as wanting to get the "real story" I went to the pub with Professor Gordon Blair, head of mechanical engineering, Belfast University, and his Irish team who ran the fabulous QUB bike. Just for the "craic" as they say. It was not a good idea at all. Not journalistically anyway.

Chapter 23

Back to speedway. Again

In speedway, Bruce Penhall had retired on the rostrum in LA after winning his second title, which left speedway in limbo without a world champion for that year. It got no better when Egon Muller, the German more famous for his long tracking, won the world title the following year in Norden, as he was not a regular British League competitor. That's not to take anything away from Egon, one of the world's truly great long track champions.

But it was Cradley Heath's own Dane, Erik Gundersen, who came to the rescue and put Danish speedway and its riders top of the pile after his win in 1984 in Gothenburg from his fellow Dane and main rival Hans Nielsen, with fellow Cradley rider, Lance King (USA), third. It was so great that Erik was a regular British League rider, where he became a well-loved ambassador for the sport, with his personality, riding ability and showmanship for all to see during his years racing so admirably in the UK.

Little Erik was a whippet of a man, quick of movement, with the quickest wit imaginable, even in his second language of English, in which he was word perfect and had everyone in tears of laughter when he perfected a superb Black Country accent, much to the delight of his adoring fans! I can still hear him say: "How yo doin', ar kid!" (Basically, how are you?)

His measure of professionalism was amazing, his bikes, his preparations were fantastic and the success which came to him was richly deserved.

Erik defended the title in 1985 and won an amazing three-man run-off at the bowl-shaped Wembley of the North, Odsal Stadium, Bradford, used for the first time after the demise of Wembley itself. Gundersen beat Nielsen and Sam Ermolenko in the vital race 21. But his day did not start well. He was very down after finishing in third spot in his first race. I had a quick word with him in the pits, as did many others, and we told him he could still do it (win the title) with four wins! And that's just what the great rider did. Four wins and a run-off victory and he was top of the world again. A great performance, well deserved.

Erik went on to win three individual world titles, the last in 1988. In 1985, Erik became the only rider to hold all four major world track titles at the same time: the world individual, World Team Cup, World Pairs and the World Long Track Championships.

But there was to be an awful crash which stopped Erik's career in full flight and almost cost him his life; that was at Bradford too. I was on reporting duty for

MCN in the pits for the World Team Cup Final at Odsal Stadium in 1989 too.

In the first race, there was an appalling collision involving Erik, Lance King, Jimmy Nilsen and Simon Cross, representing Denmark, USA, England and Sweden. It was immediately apparent that Erik had been seriously hurt. He was attended to on the track by a medical team and then was safely whisked away to hospital. The faces said it all in the pits, Erik was indeed severely injured.

The Danes were so upset at the critical condition of their star that they quite simply wanted to pull out of the meeting, which was understandable. Emotions were running high in the pits, and Erik's mechanic, traumatised at his rider's injuries, was trying to get the crashed machine into his van. On being stopped by FIM officials who had to impound the machine for examination, he practically threw the bike at them.

The meeting had to continue but the mood was sombre for the rest of the day. The press were later told that Erik's life was under threat and it was unlikely he would survive. I had to get an obituary ready in case he died, so that the terrible news would make the deadlines of the paper, but Erik was made of sterner stuff and although he never rode a speedway bike in anger again, his life was spared, and he bounced back to continue to be the life and soul of his family despite the accident taking its toll on his body. He also fought back to help up-and-coming young Danes in becoming better speedway riders.

It was one of the happiest moments in my speedway life when I was able to rip up my already prepared obituary for Erik and went on to meet him many times after that. Erik continued after his glorious career with Cradley and his international triumphs, with a great passion for teaching the young Danes the right approach to the sport. There can be no better teacher or someone to look up to. Erik is one of the very best.

1986 was smack in the middle of the Danish domination of the World Championship when Hans Nielsen won the first of his titles in Katowice, Poland, an event I missed as I was in bed with flu, unable to travel. It was the only World Final I was to miss for well over 20 years.

Nielsen was king again in 1987 in another unlikely setting for speedway with the "one-off" Final, made into a "two-day" Final in Amsterdam, Netherlands, the one and only time the shale Final went to that country or took place over two days of racing. The decision was one of finance. It was known that a non-speedway country like Holland would not attract enough spectators for a one-day event, therefore it became a two-day event to attract two crowds! It was a political move made within the corridors of the FIM. That was not the main problem, however, as the Olympic Stadium was, to a large extent, past its best. This is where speedway found itself for the showpiece event of the season and the Danes dominated it anyway, whether or not the venue was quite up to scratch.

British press quizzing the Great Dane, Ole Olsen, probably about silencers or tyres, or some such nonsense, at Vojens, Denmark, including *Speedway Star* editor, Phil Rising.

A non-speedway country running a major championship, even over the controversial two days, only attracted a total of 17,000 spectators, which must count as pretty low for any World Final run over the old "one-off" Final, which says it all really.

The points from the two days were added together to find the world champion. With 12 points on day one and a 15-point maximum on day two, Nielsen retained his crown, winning from Gundersen, three points behind on 24, who won a run-off for the place after beating Sam Ermolenko of America, who had also scored 24.

Nielsen had a very smooth style, spectacular amounts of control and was always brimming with confidence. He was a superb champion and was a great ambassador for the sport while he was top of the tree. Although he was Danish, Nielsen preferred to ride British Godden engines during his world successes, as opposed to the more generally used Italian GM or Czech Jawa.

At least Britain had a big part to play in his success, with Nielsen riding Don Godden's super motors.

Nielsen relied on his Godden power in 1988 and finished on 14 points, the same as his great rival Gundersen, on his favoured GM. In the run-off in front of a huge Danish crowd at Vojens, the venue operated by Ole Olsen, Gundersen came out on top to be crowned champion again. To complete the utter domination of the Danes, Jan O Pedersen was third on 13 points. Best Englishman was Simon Wigg, whose nine points gave him fifth place.

Munich's Olympic Stadium was chosen as the World Final venue in 1989, which was a super, modern venue unlike the Amsterdam stadium and did create a marvellous atmosphere.

The one-off track rode OK and a big crowd attended the German event which ran successfully. There was another Danish winner, however, with Nielsen winning again with a faultless 15-point maximum. Nobody could touch him after Gundersen had a rare engine failure which dropped him to fourth. Britain's Simon Wigg had his best World Speedway Final finish, ending up world runner-up to his Oxford teammate Hans with 12 points, which gave him a run-off with another Brit, Jeremy Doncaster, also on 12, which he won for the silver medal. I think Simon was nearly as proud of that finish as he was of winning all his World Long Track Finals. My recollection is that maybe Roman Matousek, the Czech and Coventry rider, found a trick way of riding the track quite late on by dropping his rear wheel inside the white line while keeping his front wheel on the track, so it was legal, both wheels not being inside the white line and a very quick way round!

Having said that, the World Final was a true reflection of a glamorous event which did the sport proud, and the atmosphere created in the modern amphitheatre of the Olympic stadium was terrific and the backstage facilities simply superb.

I remember a very good hot meal being provided for the journalists in the press room after the event, which was most acceptable. Well done for that!

With Amsterdam and Munich getting a slice of the World Final action, it was five years till the Blue Riband event came back to England for 1990. Not to Wembley, of course, which staged its last Final in 1981, but back to Bradford's Odsal Stadium, which had held its first

World Final successfully in 1985. It was the year that the Danish era came to an end after six years of their domination. It was still a Scandinavian winner though, with Swedish star Per Jonsson winning at Odsal. The steep terracing and stands helping to achieve a tremendous atmosphere for the Final. Jonsson, the darling of the Reading Racers, scored 13 points, as did American Shawn Moran, then riding for Belle Vue Aces.

A run-off was called for and Jonsson took his only well-deserved World Championship win beating Moran. It was a win which saved speedway from what would have been disastrous press. Moran was later stripped of his second place in the Final after being found guilty of failing a drug test at the Overseas Final at Coventry. Moran took painkillers which unknown to the rider were on a list of FIM banned drugs. If he had been world champion, the repercussions would have rocked the sport even more badly, with a world champion possibly banned.

Wearing super lightweight leathers from leather used for white kid gloves, Jan O Pedersen was world champion when the Final returned to one of my favourite venues in 1991, Ullevi Stadium, Gothenburg, Sweden. The Cradley Heath star rider was in a class of his own that year, winning in impeccable style with a 15-point maximum. As a rude aside, Jan O cleared the pits during practice when a particularly loud fart extricated itself through his leathers. I know, I was there. Through it all sat Jan O, now alone, with a huge smile on his face! Sorry Jan O!

Next, in runners-up spot in Ullevi, three points down was Swede Tony Rickardsson. Pedersen was a Dane, so they were top of the international standing in the sport again. It was tragic that a severe back injury only months after winning the title should end Pedersen's career. He could have gone on to win more titles, I am sure, as could Swede Jonsson, who was even more seriously hurt than Pedersen, and was left paralysed in a wheelchair after a track crash. Top Englishman in Sweden was Paul Thorp with a creditable 10 points.

The tide did change in 1992 when a precocious, dreadlocked Gary Havelock became Britain's first world champion for 12 years with a great, gritty performance in Wroclaw, Poland. He had been speedway's wild child in his formative years but was a very fine speedway rider who could live with the best of the world's talent. He divided opinion and obviously liked to have a good time away from the track, but personally, we always got on well. He was always polite and gave very sensible answers when pressed by journalists and was a truly worthy champion for Britain. He was very serious about the sport and spoke confidently with great common sense. If during an interview his wife's name came up, Havvy always said, "It's Jayne, with a y." And I've never forgotten it.

There was an intimate portrait of Gary after he won the World Championship in 92 as part of *The Inside Line* magazine by John Murphy. It's all typed out on a typewriter and features many interesting articles penned in Gary's own words. One item of particular note, and I hope they don't mind me using the words here after all these years, was being one of the first riders to use a Kevlar race suit instead of leathers.

"I wanted to try the suit on track (in practice at Bradford) as I wanted to wear it in the World Final. As things turned out it certainly proved to be a useful trial as I quickly discovered that I was sliding down the seat on the bike when I dropped the clutch, so that was no good at all really. So, we added a piece of leather around the 'seating' area of the suit which improved 'grip' drastically! The inside of the legs were burning too on the exhaust so more leather was added around the knee to stop that happening. The Kevlar suit felt strange at first, it was so very light, but also very 'stretchy'. Apparently, I'm the only speedway rider currently using a Kevlar suit, though world long track champion Marchel Gerhard has been using one."

There are two claims to fame for Gary, the first with dreadlocked hair and the first speedway world champion to use a Kevlar racing suit!

There was also a record in which Gary featured in 1992. The group Tru performed a song, "The Champ", in which Gary recited the words, during the song, "I'm the champ, I can't believe it," from an interview after he won the World Championship. Sadly, it didn't make *Top of the Pops*. I still have a copy on a cassette tape.

In the *Inside Line* issue, Gary says the engine he used at Wroclaw was the one he seized first time out during practice for the World Pairs Final in Italy. It was originally an Otto Lantenhammer tuned GM, prepared by Neil Evitts. Gary says Neil worked on the unit for four days to make sure it was ready for the Final. He used some non-durable parts, such as lightweight valves, piston and conrod which would only be strong enough to do four meetings, added Gary. "Whilst the inclusion of 'specialist' parts was significant, nothing could replace Neil's expertise in setting up the motor to run at its very best," said Gary.

His career was long and successful for club and country, including England captain, and it was a terrible shame it came to an end at Redcar when Gary suffered severe arm injuries. Nobody felt happier than I when Coventry gave him a job in speedway as the Bees team manager in 2013, later becoming promoter at Berwick.

Ever popular Sam Ermolenko took the world speedway crown for America in 1993. His win was achieved at another of speedway's unlikeliest of venues, at Pocking, in Germany, the middle of nowhere, miles away from any big city. It was more like the venue for a big grass track than the world's number one speedway meeting. But all of these "one-off" speedway finals were to be gone soon anyway. And, happily, many of the GP series venues were more high-profile stadiums in major cities than Norden or Pocking.

Chapter 24

Speedway GPs take over

Swedish superstar Tony Rickardsson became the last individual winner of the one-off finals in 1994 at Denmark's Vojens track. They were all then confined to history as a new era of Grand Prix rounds began in 1995, with six rounds being held, the first in the Olympic Stadium, Wroclaw, Poland, before a crowd of 30,000. The record books show Tomasz Gollob won that meeting and nearly caused a riot among his vociferous countrymen! The start of great Polish wins. But it was Hans Nielsen of Denmark whose consistency put him in the record books as the first world champion of the new Grand Prix style series, rather than one who was crowned after a single night's racing.

It was a controversial move and many a pundit for the "good old days" thought it was the worst idea ever, including Britain's speedway hierarchy at FIM level. But speedway had to move on. Motor racing's Formula One crown was not fought for in one day but over many rounds in many countries worldwide, and speedway was only catching up with the trends for such championships.

It has proved to be a correct choice with great coverage worldwide for the speedway championship, televised to millions in many countries, not just the UK, and making international speedway riders stars of the living room and giving maximum exposure for the riders, the sport and their sponsors.

The one-off Final was always dramatic, but speedway proved it could be just as dramatic over a series of a number of stunning GPs throughout a season. The sport stepped up to the mark and passed with flying colours. First off, Sky TV's coverage had a lot to do with its success and deserves all the ratings it gets for its outstanding shows. Since 1995, the GPs continue to roll out mega new champions with thrilling racing round after round.

I was always ecstatic at reporting on the one-off World Finals, but I am glad I was around to see the sport continue to grow into its new GP series, which visited many countries for their major championship GP round each season. The GPs helped generate more column inches of coverage than it was getting, that's for sure.

Cradley was much involved in the new era of GP racing, producing major stars. First Billy Hamill who won the Grand Prix title in 1996, followed by another Cradley star, Greg Hancock, also of America who won in 1997, albeit riding for Coventry by then!

But by 1996, the Cradley dream and that of their supporters was over. They had a year at Stoke, riding as Cradley and Stoke at Loomer Road.

It was financial disaster and lasted for only one season. I for one never wanted to see the Heathens race there, and I never went.

Dudley Wood Stadium was eventually pulled down two years later and it was to be four or five years before the land became a Barratts housing estate. The last few photos of the old stadium slowly decaying and overgrown with grass are heart-breaking for a fan who grew up in the 1960s on the terraces. Even the photographer was chased off in the end and told not to take any further pictures as he was trespassing!

Very sad sight. The derelict Cradley speedway stadium, terraces on right, burnt-out bar, with the home straight and first bend just recognisable. It was a Saturday night of dreams for years for me, my friends and thousands of others.

Gone were the days of the famous Cradley pork sandwiches being served up in the wooden café, having a pint of Watney's in the bar (yuk), especially with the late Bernard Crapper, the Oxford promoter, who was very good company. Then using the outside gent's lavatory while looking at the stars (there wasn't a roof), I think there had been a fire which burnt out the roof. A fact which made livewire journalist Dave Lanning of the *Sun* newspaper and TV commentating fame roar when he read my article describing the scene in an edition of *Vintage Magazine* many years later!

I bet you've never heard of a speedway individual meeting won with a score of 15.88. It happened at Cradley. The meeting in question took place in August 1972 and a new handicap formula devised by Cradley supremo, and a bit of an oddball, Morris Jephcott. It provided a surprise winner of the Alan Hunt Memorial Handicap trophy meeting held on a Monday night.

The winner was a reserve, Cradley's Pete Jarman, who scored seven points but won the meeting with a handicap of 8.88 added to his track score, thus giving him a winning total of 15.88!

I will explain Mr Jephcott's system. Before that, I'll say Jarman only came into the meet to replace Ronnie Moore, who had broken down en route to the track. Sixteen riders lined up and the plan was to take some of the predictability out of open meetings. The system employed was to take a rider's race average, multiply it by five, deduct the total from the 15 points it is possible to get from five rides, then add this handicap figure to the rider's final score. Phew.

The highest average rider in the line-up was world champion Ole Olsen from Wolves and he had a handicap figure of 0.95 to add to his final score. Jarman had the handicap figure of 8.88. The moral victor on the night who scored more points on the night was English international Terry Betts from King's Lynn with 13.

As Jarman had an 8.88 handicap and seven points from the track racing, he won with a combined score of 15.88. Second was Betts (1.98 handicap) plus 13 points, giving 14.98. Third was Ray Wilson (Leicester) with 2.36 handicap, plus 12 points for 14.36. Jarman won despite a fall and exclusion in his first race and exclusion again this time for tape breaking in his second outing. But with seven points from his next three completed rides, it was enough to win. If he had scored points from his first two rides, he would have won by an embarrassing margin!

As it turned out Jarman's handicap was too great, and it was said in any re-run of the experimental system the maximum amount of handicap any rider would receive would not be more than four points above the man at the other end of the scale.

But the idea was not universally accepted (at all) and could even be said to be derided, and it was never attempted again. It is one of those meetings not remembered by many except the diehard anorak person, possibly. I'd certainly forgotten the details of this bizarre experiment myself until my research into

Cradley meetings brought it to light. Now what a quiz question that would be: Who won an individual speedway meeting with a score of 15.88? Answer: Pete Jarman at Dudley Wood in 1972!

Much later, the internationally famous Coventry Brandon Stadium also closed its doors for business in a very acrimonious way. One of the most famous stadia in speedway, seemingly lost forever. Unimaginable in promoter Mr Charles Ochiltree's day. The "CO" ruling the roost from his glass-fronted gallery overlooking the pits, with nothing being missed in the whole stadium from his business-like stare. The military precision that was the hallmark of the procession which started the show, followed by the riders, was the best in the sport. It staged many great times, great meetings, championships won and lost for generations of fantastic pace and action. We saw a stadium in sad decline. But it has gone. Inconceivable for some of us oldies who remember its glory days from our youth to our seventh decade. Weekly visits remembered, although trying to get into the paddock with your car, even for a press man was like trying to get into Fort Knox to steal a bar of gold. Easier to park outside. Even when you were admitted, you sometimes had a grilling from Mrs Ochiltree in the speedway office before she'd issue you with a free programme for the press!

In my early days, the press paid to use telephones in people's houses next to the stadium to phone their offices with copy before mobile phones came on the scene!

I also remember being told off by the pits marshal for listening in to a conversation a rider was having with the referee. And later I won the 50/50 draw one year, £92 it was. A special place, a place of dreams from Jack Parker, Tommy Knudsen, Nigel Boocock, Ole Olsen and many, many others.

And that's where I can draw a line under my personal World Championship reporting days, from the first one I reported on in 1975, right through to the new GP series in 96-97.

Britain's national press talk to Bruce Penhall at an Intercontinental Final practice, Denmark. Behind my left shoulder, Mike Beale, *Daily Star*, the late Graham Baker, *Mirror*, and Keith Fisher, right, *Sunday Mirror*.

But I will include two more world champions. The first from 2000 because he is British (but Maltese born) and that's Mark Loram. I want to include Mark because he continues in the fine line of British stars who I have seen take the individual shale crown, following in the speeding tyre tracks of Peter Collins, Michael Lee and Gary Havelock. Mark came up through the old way of racing, first on junior grass track before taking up speedway, which seems now sometimes unique. Not so many of the young speedway stars tend to do much grass track these days, mainly because there aren't the meetings around now, which is a pity, if only because the likes of Peter Collins did it that way too. More recently, the latest Brit to take the number one mantle in 2013 and 2015 and 2018 is Tai Woffinden, as great and as gutsy a speedway rider as has ever been. His battles, riding with major injury to take the championship, were and still are incredible. The latest in a line of super talented British riders who have made it to the number one spot. And international stardom. His first introduction to the sport was living in a caravan at the back of the Scunthorpe pits with his family to help his speedway career. Tai deserves every success he has achieved through his own prodigious talent. His tattooed image divide's opinion but does not take away the bravery and skill that made him a multi world champion.

These are just the headline grabbers, the ones who "made it". But there are also the rest, not quite so talented perhaps, or of course, not so lucky, but who never gave up their quest to be the best they could be, who turn out, impeccably professionally, week in, week out for their teams, even when they know they will never ever be the best in their beloved sport. But without whom there would be no sport, nobody to watch, nobody to cheer on. Nobody to boo even. They are the real stars of this story. The rest. Thank you to every one of them that I have met, watched, heard about or written about; it was my pleasure. I salute you all.

Chapter 25

EastEnders!

One more story sticks out which represents how big a sport speedway was in "my" days, an era which I call my golden era. In 1997 *MCN* reported with photos the latest storyline in the major *EastEnders* BBC TV series, which revolved around speedway! Main character Ricky Butcher (played by Sid Owen) became a speedway rider with the "Walford Lions" team.

The storyline ran for a couple of months in the top-ratings show, and it was said that speedway promoters saw a big surge in interest for the shale sport after *EastEnders* became involved. The racing shots were done at Arena Essex (later Lakeside) and captain Troy Pratt did the action shots for the soap for Ricky.

The speedway storyline ran for about six weeks in the show which was regularly watched by 14 million homes. It provided the most media coverage the sport has ever seen and a massive boost to its profile.

The secret came out when filming took place at Arena Essex. Four extra races were staged for the cameras, but no soap stars were seen at the track. More filming earlier in the 97 season at Arena Essex involved more than 100 acting "extras", but it, too, was cloaked in secrecy, and speedway's bosses were forced to call it a "promotional film". The BBC even created a replica speedway pit at the show's Elstree Studios. Producers wouldn't let actor Owen ride the bike himself after former *EastEnders* actor Sean Maguire smashed his leg riding a speedway bike for the programme four years previously.

In the series, Ricky is forced to give up the sport after a crash and a tongue-lashing from his wife Bianca, alias actress Patsy Palmer.

That just shows how big a deal speedway was in those days, to get the most talked-about TV show to publicise the sport.

Because the sport was so big, some distinctly non-speedway venues were tried out, some good, some which worked, some which were not so good. Some were one-offs or didn't last long, but in those far-off days, anything could be given a go.

Just before I joined *MCN*, in around 1971 to 73, former Cradley rider Harry Bastable promoted what he called Speedtrack, indoor racing at the famous Granby Halls, Leicester, and Whispering Wheels skating rink, Temple Street, Wolverhampton. It was a peculiar sport, with riders mounted on 175cc BSA two-stroke Bantams in a speedway style frame, sorted by Rob Homer. Because the floor was wood, riders had to wear not a steel shoe on their left boot but a felt carpet slipper to help the foot slide!

Bastable said: "Those poor Bantams were given a fistful no other poor Bantam had ever dreamed of!" Bike designer Homer won the Midland Individual Riders' Championship three days before Christmas in 1971, beating Arthur Browning by one point. Seeing six-foot speedway Brummie star Arthur ride a tiny Bantam was something else.

There was a mixture of speedway, grass track, and scramblers involved, including Harry's son, Steve Bastable, James Bond, trials man John Gaskell, Geoff Bouchard, Chris Harrison, Terry Challinor, scrambler, and grasser Cyril Jones.

Many meetings were held at the venue on Monday or Tuesday nights starting at 8pm and included fixtures like four team tournaments; Leicester v Birmingham v Wolverhampton v Midland Pirates, Leicester took on a Midland Select, Sprite American Eagle, Wolverhampton Wasps and the Birmingham Bombers. On 19 February 1973, the four-lap track record was 47 seconds by Gordon Bowden. I did attend the meetings several times, but because of the constricted nature of the track and the use of tiny motorcycles, it was hardly that dramatic, but a very good attempt at something new and unique which lasted for a time. Trouble was the spectators were limited to 300.

The Leicester team manager was Vic White and visiting team manager was ex-Cradley man Ted Flanaghan. It could in no way be called speedway and was an entertainment, similar in idea to the winter indoor Telford ice rink meetings held so successfully by Ian Thomas and Graham Drury for many years later on.

Granby Halls was the unlikely home of noisy motorcycle racing; it was normally a well-known roller rink venue which also hosted rock concerts, including the Rolling Stones, Cream and Yes and was the home of the oldest operating basketball team in the country, the Leicester Riders from 1981–2000. The Halls have now been pulled down and are now a car park.

It was not the first time that the title "speedtrack" had been used in the UK; in the 1970s the Lydden track in Kent ran international "speed track" events, like a big grass track for both solos and sidecars, promoted by the Astra club.

Motor Cycle News sponsored the International Long Track Race of the Year four years later at Chasewater Raceway, Brownhills, West Midlands on Sunday, April 17, at 2pm.

This was another non-motorcycling venue and held pony-trotting races, which started on Monday, 16 August 1971. The meeting was the brainchild of Dave Owen and the FTRC on behalf of Chasewater Promotions at Chasewater Stadium. I was there to cover our meeting in 1977, which attracted a star-studded field of riders.

It was a full bonanza of oval track racing and included a solo Bahn record as held at German long track meetings, a Great Britain v Rest of the World team match, the beautiful-sounding 750cc Triumph Strongbow solos and sidecars too. It was a fantastic meeting.

Super Swede Anders Michanek won the Bahn record, one flying lap of the track, with 25.8 seconds, followed by Ivan Mauger in 26.2s, Peter Collins 26.4s, and Egon Muller and Dave Morton both on 27s.

A Great Britain side team managed by Lew Coffin lost to a Rest of the World squad with *Speedway Star* editor Phil Rising as team manager. There were six-man races, with scoring from six points for a win down to one. GB were Peter Collins, Don Godden, Malcolm Simmons, Dave Jessup, Mike Beaumont, Tom Leadbitter, Chris and Dave Morton, and Malc Corradine, reserve.

The world side was Ivan Mauger, Ole Olsen, Anders Michanek, Egon Muller, Kristian Praestbro (Christian Preastbro in programme), Barry Briggs, and Ila Teromaa, reserve.

The Triumph Bonneville flat trackers were ridden by Chippy Moore, Malc Corradine, Barry Robinson, Rob Lidgate, Ted Hubbard and Paul Pinfold.

Sidecar men were Steve Smith, Alan Artus, Roger Measor, Gordon Matthews and Paul Pinfold.

After the team match heats, semi-finals and a Final were held for the solos. Ole Olsen won the first semi, then the Final. It proved to be the last motorcycle race held at Chasewater.

There was a good crowd, and it must have been a success, but local opposition on the grounds of noise meant another meeting was never held at the trotting track.

The oval shape of the track can still be seen on Google Earth maps, which now lies next to the M6 toll booths, and is part of Chasewater Heaths site of special scientific interest.

There was another unusual setting for a British long track in 1978 on the Devon and Exeter horse racecourse. Long Track Racing Associates, with Peter Oakes meeting secretary and one of the prime movers behind the bold new venture, set out a purpose-built long track on the site which was called the Haldon long track arena. The half-mile shale track had been specially laid down by long-time British speedway promoter Maurice Morley and Sid Stone. It had nice long straights, but the complaint was that the bends were more like tighter speedway turns than wider continental long tracks.

They held an international on Sunday, October 8, and a star-quality line-up was attracted to the new venue. Action started with a Bahn rekord, a flying lap from five of the competitors, timed individually. Peter Collins was the fastest, completing his lap in 27.61 seconds, followed by Norwegian Open long track champion Reidar Eide, 27.69s, America's top speedway rider Scott Autrey 27.79s, England international Dave Jessup 27.83s and Peter's brother Les Collins 28.09s.

Each rider took six rides in the 16-race individual format. First race that day was won by Reading speedway's Bernie Leigh after a thrilling battle with Norwegian Tormod Langli, who rode for Bristol, Doug Wyer third, John Davis fourth, Mike Beaumont fifth and Les Collins last.

Experienced long tracker Eide was successful in a tight finish when he had to win his last race to win the title, which he did from Peter Collins, Vaclav Verner, Wyer and reserve Bob Watts.

It meant Aussie Phil Crump had to be content with runner-up place.

Haldon was back the following year to stage their second meeting. Initially, Long Track Racing Associates had hoped to stage a qualifying round off the World Long Track Championship on Sunday, May 13 but unfortunately had to withdraw their application when the winter weather made it impossible to carry out all the alterations demanded by the FIM, the controlling body of motorcycle sport.

But a full international field was assembled, including American Bruce Penhall, who was in his second year of racing over here, with Cradley Heath US star Autrey again, plus Great Dane Ole Olsen, Kiwi star Larry Ross, Czech international Jiri Stancl, plus Brits Phil Collins and Doug Wyer.

This time it was Crump, runner-up the previous year, who took top honours. The former Australian long track champion put in an astonishing performance and remained unbeaten in his six rides to get a perfect score of 30 points. Penhall took a liking to the track and had three wins in his 25-points haul.

Haldon was back on September 30 that same year with an even bigger coup! They had as their star turn sensational American dirt track champion and 500cc world road race champion Kenny Roberts competing in a couple of Transatlantic challenge races.

The three-page article called "The Roberts Magic Show" and my intro read, "World road race champ Kenny Roberts made his British dirt track debut on the half-mile Haldon long track – by popping 80mph wheelies down the start/finish straight, to the delight of the 15,000 crowd."

Promoters Bruce Cox and Gavin Trippe provided a field of eight American-style 750cc dirt trackers. Roberts' own Yamaha machine was flown in specially for the occasion, along with master tuner Shell Thuett, who helped Kenny to his two American national titles on the dirt. Cox constructed seven of his own machines and brought them over to the UK. It was said the cost of building the machines and shipping was over £20,000.

Adding spice to the challenge was American Dave Aldana, wearing his famous, at one time banned, "skeleton" leathers, with the human skeleton picked out in white on black leathers. Best set of leathers ever in bike racing. Aldana was one of the stars of the great *On Any Sunday* motorcycle racing film and was a brilliant dirt and road racer, being at one time a works rider for BSA, Norton, Suzuki, Kawasaki and Honda. Highlight of the supertracker event was the Toshiba Transatlantic Supertracker challenge in which Roberts, Aldana, and fellow American speedway rider Kelly Moran battled with Britain's Peter and Les Collins and Richard "Chippy" Moore, also on the big twins.

Just the sight and sound of the four-stroke Yamaha twins on one wheel down the straights in the hands of Roberts and Dave Aldana, captain of the US Transatlantic road race series this year, was alone enough to justify the entrance money.

The big head-to-head challenge between British champion Peter Collins on a 500cc works Weslake and Roberts on a 750cc works Yamaha dirt track was an intriguing encounter.

Collins was inside Roberts, for the star was a fraction quicker off the gate than the heavier Yamaha and that proved a decisive factor. Collins opened up a four-second lead and despite Roberts keeping both wheels on the ground this time out, he was unable to cut back Collins' lead.

The first time out for five of the Yamaha dirt tracks came in the Toshiba Transatlantic challenge when Roberts electrified the crowd with his antics with Aldana. In the early stages of the five lapper, Chippy Moore was right up with them, but he slid off on the pits turn. Best placed Englishman was Les Collins, in third ahead of brother Peter who dropped back when he felt the Yamaha engine seizing.

Roberts completed a double when he took the Toshiba Daily Mirror Supertrack Grand Slam Final from the ever-improving Moore. Les Collins also quickly mastering the technique of riding the heavy Yamahas (compared to British speedway bikes) finished third, while visiting America Aldana had back luck. Involved in a terrific dice with Roberts for the lead, he inadvertently pulled out his engine cut out lead – and finished the race holding the cut out on the right handlebar with his left hand while still lapping very quickly!

The cold and damp weather at Haldon attempted to spoil the day but Roberts produced that magic show for the fans, which will be long remembered by those who saw it.

Roberts, who wore the US dirt track style boots with laces up the front said: "I haven't done dirt track for a couple of years, but this sort of racing gives me more thrills than racing a road bike." And Haldon? "It's a little small. We have about 75bhp are going faster down the straights but the bends are small. Here we are using third and fourth gears, while on the bigger American tracks we use fifth."

Aldana said: "It's a good surface here, just like back home on the horse race tracks, but our bends are three times as wide as this."

Roberts travelled in style during his stay in Devon, having a Mercedes Benz car placed at his disposal by Dunns Motors.

The announcer called Kenny Roberts, Kenny Stevens on the first lap! But the Yamaha riders did race with completely different numbers from those printed in the programme, confusing for newcomers to dirt track, and there were plenty of road racing fans at this meeting.

The show was a great event for Britain which unfortunately has never been replicated.

There was a national part of the programme for long track bikes, and it was Australian international Phil Crump who won his second major competition at Haldon. He won from Cradley and New Zealand international Bruce Cribb second, Czech international Vaclav Verner third, British grass track Chris Baybutt fourth, Les Collins fifth and Trevor Banks sixth in the Final.

The last meeting was I believe 29 June 1980, which was won by Andy Grahame with Steve Bastable runner-up and Kenny Carter third. Poor crowds were one of the reasons why the plug was pulled on the venue, which was rumoured to be the site of a new Exeter speedway track after the sad closure of the County Ground.

Chapter 26

Honda speedway engine

I tried to champion the association between former England speedway rider Eric Boocock and top international road racer and TT star and Isle of Man record holder Mick Grant, who tried to get Honda engines into speedway in the 1990s. The pair of them put so much hard work into that worthy project it is a travesty that it all came to nothing. It was a grand idea at the time, and Grant with his mechanical know-how, produced a Honda-engined speedway bike from a stock Honda engine, which would have been much cheaper to run for riders, especially in any second tier of league racing or a special one-off series.

There was a complete lack of goodwill for Honda from the sports bosses in my opinion and, from my point of view, it was hard to take. Because Honda are the world's biggest motorcycle manufacturer, market leader and one of the greatest engineering businesses in the world. I believe through Mick Grant and Eric Boocock they were trying to help speedway. But it was a failure. And I know both Grant and Boocock were furious.

Speedway was not ready for such a ground-changing idea. It was too revolutionary for the insular sport. I give but two examples; I was at Peterborough during a match where all riders were on Hondas as a test for the engines and it was going well. I thought the spectacle would come, even if it was used only as a kind of stepping-stone for the younger rider to get a foothold into the sport, before having to go and equip himself with expensive GM or Jawa engines.

The top man at Honda UK was in the pits at Peterborough, it might have been Bob McMillan, and he was left entirely on his own. No British promoters, no riders, no officials, nobody was talking to him. I knew from them on it was doomed.

I was also told by a very good source that at another meeting with the Honda bikes, some were taken to the back of the pits and most of the oil poured out, hoping they would seize! If that is true, it was misguided and very small-minded. It would seem there were riders, some promoters and others concerned in the sport who didn't want Honda involved, which was tragic to me. What other sports discipline would have declined Honda's help? Speedway did.

I was upset when the project folded up. Maybe, looking back, it was not the full answer, but I'm afraid it showed speedway up for being pretty petty and not at all progressive. I do understand that the traditional speedway engine manufacturers like GM, Jawa etc. and the tuners would have been under threat from the idea because they make their money off the riders. However, I would have thought, hoped, that a way forward could have been discovered whereby these manufacturers could have been protected and indeed could have changed their products to include a standard engine for rookie and clubmen type riders to keep the costs down while still providing for most of the other riders in the sport, the professional star men riding the 'full on' engines. Historically, it has always been difficult for youngsters starting out in the sport because of the expense of very specialised equipment. The Honda project had simply tried to help.

I do fear there are two distinct sides to speedway these days. There are the glamorous, well-represented Grand Prix and international championships supported, encouraged and publicised so well by TV, first Sky and Eurosport, then BT Sport, and they produce a superb package whereby speedway comes over excitingly well and plays to a thrilled audience of thousands worldwide.

But at the grass-roots level, when I go to see Premiership and Championship racing in this country, the crowd numbers have plummeted.

How on earth can such clubs survive supported only by possibly less than 1,000 spectators for a match while they ride middle and lower order foreigners, paying their flights in and out of the country each time they race. It is untenable. I do fear for club closures, but I do hope I am proved wrong. But also, while speedway uses the guest rider rules on such a grand scale and the farcical sight of riders riding for two clubs, in my opinion, is wrong. We must find more riders from our own resources. Although, from a rider's point of view, riding for two teams makes economic sense and a way to make a living from the sport. I do see that.

Therefore, I did hope f2 speedway envisaged by former Peterborough rider Pete Seaton would be given a better run by the sport than when Honda became involved.

It was Pete's idea for a cheaper, enduro-engined speedway bike to be produced in some numbers, which would make it easier for riders to cut their teeth in the sport and to be able to run a bike that would be cheap to run for an entire season, with bulletproof clutches, for instance, which would last longer than having to be stripped every meeting like current speedway machines.

Pete's f2 idea had the great advantage that it was not one-make based. It encapsulates Kawasaki, Honda, BMW, all sorts of manufacturers, who produce the practically bulletproof 450cc enduro/supermoto style four-stroke single engines which are readily available, and which will slot into traditional speedway frames without much fuss and will give the rider a good speedway feel while racing on small shale ovals. All without breaking the bank.

I for one hoped the f2 would become a standalone championship starting out at clubman level. Pete's death in 2020 may well have closed the promising idea, but I hope not.

Chapter 27

MCN stars of four decades

In 1995 at *MCN*, we were all involved in a project to rate the world's greatest bike sport superstars to celebrate four decades of action in *MCN*'s time 1955–1995.

Lists like these are always controversial, but the number one would still be the same now I reckon, because we announced in the paper Mike Hailwood MBE as the number one over those 40 years.

As expected from a newspaper mainly covering road racing, the top 10 were all road race heroes. They were Giacomo Agostini second, Barry Sheene MBE third, Geoff Duke fourth, Jarno Saarinen fifth, Freddie Spencer sixth, John Surtees MBE seventh, Phil Read eighth, Kenny Roberts ninth, Carl Fogarty tenth.

Speedway was well represented with Ivan Mauger OBE MBE the six-time world champion in eleventh place, which was a fantastic achievement. Next up in twelfth place came Wayne Rainey, while thirteenth spot was held by another speedway man Peter Collins MBE, 1976 world champion.

The rest of the list from 14th to 40th reads like a who's who too. In order, they are Eddie Lawson, Joey Dunlop MBE, Kevin Schwantz, Dave Thorpe, Jim Redman MBE, Bill Ivy, Jordi Tarres, Jock Taylor, Ove Fundin, Cal Rayborn, Barry Briggs MBE, Jeremy McGrath, Angel Nieto, Jean-Michel Bayle, Rolf Biland, Eric Geboers, Steve Webster MBE, Rick Johnson, Bruce Penhall, Stephane Peterhansel, Roger De Coster, Joel Robert, Jeff Smith, Michael Lee, Simon Wigg, Sammy Miller.

What memories a list like that invokes. With seven speedway men in that list, along with mighty road racers, motocross and trials riders, I reckon the shale men held their own in such great company.

Charts were a great part of *MCN* and came in handy when I was asked to edit the *Motor Cycle News* pocket diary printed and published by Charles Letts & Co Ltd in collaboration with the paper. I started as editor of the diary in the mid-70s and held the job into the 90s. I banged in every chart I could to fill up the editorial pages of the diary, past winners of the *Motor Cycle News* Man of the Year, Machine of the Year, world road racing champions, motocross and speedway's roll of honour. In the 80s, I chose eight bikes from our *MCN* test file with a "mini test" for each bike; in 1988 these included the Honda NS125, Suzuki TSX125, Yamaha TZR250, Yamaha RD350LC, Yamaha XT600, BMW K75S, Ducati 750F1, Honda VFR750, Kawasaki GTR1000 and Suzuki GSX-R1100. I got the road test lads to do me a one-paragraph summary of all the bikes and a performance chart with standing quarter mile and top speed. It was all good publicity for the newspaper, and I was able to say: *MCN*, first with full tests of new bikes; *MCN* leads the field in putting every new model through its paces.

I can still remember the buzz I used to get each year when I went into W H Smith's newsagents as soon as the new diary came out each year, to see my name as editor on the first page. My mum used to get the first one from me and she used her copy year in, year out as her own diary of events, many of which I still have. The diary must have sold well as Charles Letts kept publishing it for many years. I think I was supposed to do the editorial for the diary out of hours, at home, but if memory serves, I found the time to do it during office hours, although I was paid extra for doing the editorial job with the diary.

The *MCN* diary followed on from a Letts "Motor Cycling" diary. I have one from 1967 which reflected the ever-changing shape of the world of motorcycles. In that little pocket tome, there is a trade directory of British Motorcycle Manufacturers including AJS, Bond cars, BSA, Cotton, DMW, Dot (Devoid of Trouble!), Excelsior, Enfield (Redditch), Francis Barnett, Greeves, James, Matchless, Scott, Veloce, Isetta, Reliant, all now long gone in an ever-changing world of bikes.

There were photos to be chosen for the inside and back pages and a selection of the year's best photos from the office files to be chosen for my diary. To start with, the diary had been plain dark blue or red, but an innovation for the 80s was a colour sticker on the front of the diary, which was much better and eye-catching in a shop. When it became worn, it could be peeled off, exposing the *MCN* logo underneath. I see in 1979 it cost £1.10 but by 1986 had become £2.95, but still a lovely Christmas present stocking filler for the readers of *MCN*.

Chapter 28

More *MCN* changes

In the mid-90s, the way speedway was reported changed at *MCN*. The sport was lumped together with all "Off Road" sport in the paper. My name appeared on the logo, "Speedway and grass track" but also "Off Road" by me as well.

I was responsible for stories concerning World Championship motocross, World Championship trials and gossip from both. In 1996/97 *MCN* became more short, sharp *Sun* newspaper style and as many stories as possible had to be "world scoops", "world exclusives", "first" pictures unveiled of new bikes etc. It was up to me to come up with or least organise such stories for *MCN*.

I think I had a good shot at it, despite being taken out of my "comfort zone" of speedway. For instance, under my by-line, *MCN* had world-exclusive photos of the four-stroke YZ400 moto-crosser, which was spread over most of two pages with the strapline: "The YZ400F uses the most advanced four-stroke engine that Yamaha has ever produced." The YZM400 Yamaha had been a sensation in motocross but the production version we revealed was also going to be revolutionary for the sport. *MCN* unveiled its full spec for our readers, including a photo of the five-valve head.

I wrote that the launch of the 400 Yamaha would host a number of rivals to make new four-strokes including a 400 from Honda and the other major Japanese manufacturers, which it did.

We were so helped by the fantastic world talent that the UK still had in those days. My byline was on an *MCN Sport* front page detailing the first world indoor trials win of legendary Yorkshire rider Dougie Lampkin in '97. Dougie's first of many world titles came in Monaco, and later that same year he won his first outdoor world title. Unfortunately, I was not sent to cover the first one in the principality.

His victory came after a thrilling win over Spanish rival Marc Colomer. Dougie took the title in dramatic fashion, which was described by me for our *MCN* trials followers, of which there were many. The Yorkshire ace took the title after two tie-breaks to decide the championship at the final round.

The win was a "royal" one too, as looking on were members of Monaco's royal family. It was sweet revenge for Dougie who had been pipped to the world outdoor title by Colomer in 1996. He became Britain's first world trials champion for more than 20 years.

His father, Martin, had won world glory in 1975. Dougie celebrated his 21st birthday two days after winning the title.

1997 was the first year of the FIM World Indoor Trials Cup and was a huge success right from the start. The British round at Sheffield Arena attracted 10,000 fans.

Martin Lampkin's 1975 title came in the first world trials championship too, before that championships had only European status. Proud dad Martin was ecstatic to have been the first world trials champion and son Dougie to have clinched the first world indoor trials crown and outdoor too.

I visited the Lampkin's family home for a feature on Dougie, and I was made at home and had a lovely day. *MCN* did some riding shots on typical gruelling Yorkshire sections. I did do plenty of trials coverage, but not as far as Monaco, but did get to World Championship rounds at Hawkstone Park, Shropshire.

How on earth the world's best trials riders got through and up near-vertical sections was a big eye-opener. These lads were super talented on these tricked-up, lightweight motorcycles, absolutely awe-inspiring.

I was sent to cover world motocross for *MCN* too. In 1997 it was off to Foxhill, Wilts, along with 20,000 spectators. The report and massive photos from *MCN* staff photographer John "Selwyn" Noble covered three pages of the paper on Wednesday.

For Brit Paul Malin, the meeting was a disaster. The factory Yamaha rider failed to qualify for the 125 races as he struggled with two broken bones in his right foot. He had picked up the injury at the British championship round only the week before in Culham, Oxon. At Foxhill, Malin finished 24th in his qualifying group, just outside the top 20 qualifying spot.

It was also amazing to see one of the all-time legends of motocross Stefan Everts ride at Foxhill. The Belgian star was in sparkling form and won his third British GP in a row in the 250s. I wrote: "Rivals found the reigning world champion too hot to handle in the sizzling sunshine at the Wiltshire circuit. Everts won both races on his factory Honda."

Everts said: "I just love the big crowds at Foxhill. In the first few laps of the race, all I could hear was the fantastic noise of the horns and the fans cheering, it completely drowns out the noise of the engines." I remember it was a fantastic event and the atmosphere was brilliant being so close to all those cheering motocross superfans. It was not such a good feeling for Justin Morris. The RWJ Silkolene Honda rider was hurt when his right leg was flung back after he hit a massive bump on the Wiltshire circuit. His leg went backwards and came down on the end of the silencer tailpipe which jammed into his upper thigh. He didn't crash but pulled up in agony. Doctors had to insert 40 stitches in his right leg. Practice was stopped while Justin received medical attention trackside. He did appear at Foxhill for the race day, but only in a role to sign autographs. He is just one more racing hero I came across in my long reporting career. Amazing people. So driven. I always was humbled by such dedication to their sport and their handling of tough situations when things went wrong on two wheels.

Later that year, I was off to report on the British Open GP at Hawkstone Park, Shropshire.

More than 6,000 fans packed Hawkstone, but for Brit hero Kurt Nicoll that day was a disaster. A freak accident when the seat of his KTM bike broke off forced him to retire from race one. Nicoll bravely fought back to clinch third place in the second race.

Nicoll was fifth in the first race when his seat worked loose and then ripped off completely when both brackets sheared, which forced him out of the race. While Nicoll cursed his luck, the event was won by Belgium's Joel Smets on a Husaberg.

While the Hawkstone event covered almost two pages with five photos, round three of the Speedway GP series at Landshut, Germany, had five short paragraphs recording the win by Hans Nielsen of Denmark. It was the sign of the times for several years.

But world exclusives under the Off-Road banner continued with the first picture and details of the ground-breaking 1998 aluminium-framed CR125 Honda moto-crosser.

It used a twin-spar road bike style frame, first seen on the CR250, 12 months before. It was also given a five-speed close-ratio gearbox.

In the same issue, speedway did have five stories and a photo. The photo showed a triumphant return to Cornwall after a break of 34 years of a speedway track cut into a quarry at St Austell. The first race was between new amateur league club St Austell Gulls and Western Warriors, which drew a crowd of 3,000.

The stadium at the Clay Country Parc, Longstone Pit, Nanpean, saw the Gulls lose 36–41. The last meeting in Cornwall had been at the Par Stadium, St Austell in September 1963.

My contacts in America came up with the goods for *MCN* in January 1997 when we had not only a world exclusive but "scoop" photos of motocross legend Jeremy McGrath testing a new Suzuki in the US.

The world's number one rider tried the RM250 days before the start of the US super cross season in Los Angeles, California. It was a big scoop for McGrath who was a Honda legend, we had a photo of him actually testing a rival Suzuki. On the same page, another "scoop". This time we unveiled Yamaha's first ever four-stroke moto-crosser, an all-new liquid-cooled YZM400F. The bike was designed to take the Japanese giant to glory in the Open World Championship and American racing.

All these scoops weekly, and you can begin to see why some punters, some tongue in cheek, called *MCN* "a comic"! But *MCN* always had the last laugh, the company was making money hand over fist and gave me my living for all those years!

Innovation and clever features were always *MCN*'s name of the game. When I was in charge of Off Road, we had the idea of explaining the awesome technique involved in super cross jumps. We found the biggest jump in the country at Britain's first purpose-built super-cross training track at Sittingbourne, Kent and asked off-road racer Warren Edwards (no relation) how it was done, and our *MCN* photographer Howard Boylan came along to capture the sensational action with his cameras.

It was a fantastic day watching the talented crosser Warren do his stuff, me sometimes standing in the valley of the massive jump with Warren soaring away above my head. Fantastic.

The country's biggest jump was a scary three-humped monster with an incredible 27m (90ft) leap, designed by Warren himself. It was an obstacle only experienced riders should tackle so I asked Warren to talk us through the spectacular jump. He said: "Stand on top of the take off ramp, which has a severe 30-degree angle, and imagine yourself going over the jump. Go over every detail again and again in your mind until you feel very confident. The last corner before the jump is 20m (62.6ft) away from the first hump and banked. I make my approach to take off in third gear. About three quarters of the way round the turn I peel off the banking to give me about 6m (20ft) of straight line run up.

"With the bike in third I accelerate smoothly towards the jump. I aim for a take-off speed of around 45mph. But it's not just the speed that will carry you over. Good technique is just as important. As I get to within about 3m (10ft) from lift off I stand up and get my body balanced. Then I increase speed to the top of the take off point.

"Just as the front wheel leaves the ramp, I roll off the throttle and the bike leaves the ground. As long as everything goes well this is a chance to relax for a few seconds and enjoy the flight. Then it's time to think about the landing.

"You want to come down at the same angle as the down slope for the smoothest possible landing. So, as you are in the air you need to adjust the angle of the bike. You can do that by dabbing the back brake. When you take off the rear wheel is obviously spinning at speed and that pulls the back of the bike down in flight. Slow the wheel down and the front drops more.

"If you've done this right, the landing should be smooth. When you hit the deck, accelerate hard down the straight and on to the next obstacle."

It was great to be involved in such an amazing leap of faith by Warren. I enjoyed it and I reckon my readers did too, it was a spectacular two-page colour *MCN* feature, with fantastic photos to go with it. Out of the top draw, even for *MCN*!

Warren's track record for showing us how it was done was outstanding. At the time, he rode for Britain's Wiseco Honda 250 squad, but his credentials included 1996 German super cross runner-up, in 1989 he was second overall at the NEC super cross, Birmingham, in 1992 he was fifth overall on a Yamaha in his first 500 World Championship race in America. He was Portuguese super cross champion in 1993–94 and in 1994 he was second in the German super cross championship, third in 1995 and second in 1996.

Chapter 29
My era 1973-98

I began to think of all the British world champions there had been during my era at *MCN* from 1973-98, and lots of great names came to mind. Here's some of them. It's not a complete record of their greatness, some riders went on to win other titles after my arbitrary cut-off year of 1998.

As it was *MCN*'s major sport, we look first at road racing. It was in 1973 that Phil Read showed us that British is best when he took the world 500cc road race championship for MV Agusta, and always a difficult trick, he retained the title again the following year in 1974. The "Prince of Speed" MBE was the first man to win world championships in the 125, 250 and 500 classes. We had to wait, but not too long for the emergence of the one and only, the great Barry Sheene to take the 500-world crown in 1976 with Suzuki, and he too repeated the Read trick and retained the coveted title in 1977. That same year George O'Dell took the world sidecar crown, passengered by first Kenny Arthur then Cliff Holland. He was a legend in that the last time a British driver had won a World Championship was in 1953 by Eric Oliver. O'Dell was the first driver to lap at over 100mph at the Isle of Man

TT the year he won his World Championship. O'Dell died under very tragic circumstances in a house fire in 1981.

There were some great three-wheeler men in my era. Next up for a world crown was Scot Jock Taylor and Benga Johansson, who won in 1980. I believe fellow Scot and *MCN* chief reporter Norrie Whyte had a soft spot for Taylor. He was indeed a four-time TT winner and set a lap record of 108.29mph in 1982 which stood for seven years. He died later that year in the Finnish GP at Imatra.

Steve Webster and Tony Hewitt came on the scene and were the undisputed kings of the three-wheel drifters by winning world titles in 1987, 1988 and 1989. It was that man Webster who won again in 1991 accompanied by passenger Gavin Simmons. At the finish of his career, Webster had won 10 sidecar titles.

The great list of sidecar drivers continued during my time at *MCN* with Darren Dixon and Andy Hetherington, winners of the world top spots in 1995 and 1996. He was also a solo rider of great merit too; he won the British F1 championship on a Suzuki in 1988 and had two GP 500 starts.

But there're even more number ones on two wheels. The Formula TT brought us some great champions too from 1977 when it was Phil Read, followed in 1978 by Mike Hailwood (in his legendary comeback year) winning on his Sports Motorcycles of Manchester Ducati 900SS and 1979 by Ron Haslam. Joey Dunlop dominated the event, winning each year from 1982–1986. The great names continued with Carl Fogarty in 1988–89, the rider with the scariest blue eyes of all time! It was Fogarty who was top of the pile for Britain in the World Superbike category in 1994, 1995 and 1998. The world endurance title came in 1992 for Terry Rymer/Carl Fogarty for Kawasaki. Foggy MBE was a four-time World Superbike champion. He broke the Isle of Man TT outright lap record in 1992 on a Yamaha 750 at a speed of 123.61mph which stood for seven years, a remarkable feat. Simply, he was one of the most successful World Superbike riders of all time. Top of the list. Legendary Ducati man. Never one to shy away from controversy, Wikipedia states: "He frequently voiced his opinion (most often in the British motorcycle newspaper, *MCN*)." But the fans loved him, his fast, hard-riding style at the TT where he had legendary races and the world superbikes. He won the *I'm a Celebrity, Get Me Out of Here* TV show in 2014.

Notably the motocross world list starts with Graham Noyce, who won the 500cc dirt title in 1979 on his Hondas. He was the first British rider to win the 500 title since Jeff Smith (BSA) in 1965. It was not until 1985 that Britain again won the 500 motocross world crown, this time through Dave Thorpe (Honda) with no less than three titles, 1985, 1986 and 1989 In 1981, Neil Hudson (Yamaha) also reigned as 250 world champion.

Wins in the Motocross des Nations were few and far between, but the fantastic feat was managed in 1994 by a trio of Kurt Nicoll, Rob Herring and Paul Malin, in

Roggenburg, Switzerland. The des Nations, dubbed the Olympics of motocross, had previously been won by GB in 1967 in the Netherlands through Dave Bickers, Vic Eastwood and Jeff Smith, and GB also won in 1966, 1965, 1964 and 1963.

In world trials, during my era, the mantle fell upon Martin Lampkin in 1975, which was the inaugural world title, after being previously called the European. Martin had won the Euro and British titles, and also won the world-famous Scott trial four times and the Scottish Six Days Trial three times.

Then came his son, Dougie Lampkin MBE, winner of the trials crown in 1997, the first of seven consecutive world trials championships to 2003. Dougie won five consecutive indoor trials championships (1997–2001), four world team championships (Trial des Nations), 1997, 1999, 2002 and 2003. He, like his father, won the Scott trial four times. He won the Scottish Six Days Trial 11 times.

Top 125 enduro man in 1990 was Paul Edmondson, again in 1993 and 1994 with an over 175 crown in 1996. I enjoyed talking to Paul, when he was based in America, to get first-hand reports of his great wins and I helped with a couple of features later in the UK. He told me once he ran out of fuel in America during a competition and shouted to the crowd for a can of petrol. Blank looks, until he realised and started to shout gas, gas, which the American understood, not petrol, and I believe some was found! A regular in the

British team in the International Six Days Enduro (ISDE) with a record 16 Gold Medals.

In world long track, a sign of greatness is when a rider can win both the 1,000 metre and speedway disciplines. One of those men was Brit Michael Lee, who took the shale crown in 1980 and the long track title in 1981. But the king of the long track was Simon Wigg who took titles in 1985, 1989, 1990, 1993 and 1994. That world title was also won by Kelvin Tatum in 1995, now a highly regarded TV pundit.

World speedway crowns were held by Peter Collins, 1976, Michael Lee, 1980, Gary Havelock, 1992, a trio of wins which I was delighted to see and report on personally, from Poland twice and Sweden once.

World junior speedway titles came UK's way in 1990 through Chris Louis and in 1993 Joe Screen. There were five World Team Cup wins for GB in 1973, 1974, 1977, 1980 and 1989.

That list includes some of the greatest British names of motorcycle racing, on tarmac and off road, be it in trials, motocross, enduro, and speedway. And *MCN* was always there to record all their great achievements! Some of them even by me!

Chapter 30

Life after *MCN*.

I decided to take early retirement from *MCN* in 1996.

Not a complicated tale really. I had been travelling around the country and the world on a regular basis, mainly at weekends, when I came to the conclusion there was another life to be tried outside of the rigours of a weekly regime of *MCN*, which over many years had changed, not much for the better if I am honest.

It was a bit free and easy when I joined. There was one golden, unwritten rule; get the job finished first, then nobody minded if you perhaps came in a bit late, went home a bit early, had a long, extended lunch break, coffee break, as long as no one could ring you up and slag you off that irate sub-editors were still waiting for your copy.

Some editors were great, really good people, some editors were not, and in their little ways gave me a bit of a hard time, I thought. It came down to this really. I had had a great time doing a job I liked, the best job in the world for me, which gave me a life that would make every other speedway pundit and fan green with envy. I had been doing it for 23 years, seen 21 World Speedway

Finals, reported on the Grand Prix Series, reported World Long Track Finals, World Ice Speedway Finals, World Team Cup finals, World Pairs Finals, British Grass Track Finals, World and British Motocross and Trials Championships, the Isle of Man TT, even the Macau road race off the coast of China. I had my reports and features published thousands of times under my by-line. Seen the world for free. Been paid for it.

But I had basically stopped in the same job. Because I loved it. The consequence of this was that I was getting older, while those in power, the generals and sometimes petty lieutenants above me in the office hierarchy, were getting younger. Not a situation I found to my liking. I felt more regimented, hours became stricter, taking time out for a cup of tea for elevenses and even going out for lunch breaks were frowned upon, and going home at exactly the set going-home time seemed out of the question. Much background tut-tutting in the way that only office workers know. No matter that some of the staff had played about all day, having a laugh, doing no work at all, only to get heads down at 5.30pm and start hammering out work at their desks until early evening, which went down really well with some kinds of editor, who were fooled. For me, I wanted another life. A life I could call my own. Some journos preferred the office and did not seem to want to go home at all. Maybe, I was wrong, too regimented in my own mind. But I'm afraid I was not one for turning, and all these years later, I stand by what I did and why I did it. I have no regrets.

Inevitably *MCN* had changed. Their attitude to speedway had changed. They didn't really want to know about the sport. I became the off-road editor, covering anything from world trials to motocross meetings and, just like that, it seemed to me, was expected to come up with sensational, headline-grabbing stories about sports which I knew about but did not know the main players, like I did in speedway. This made life for me a bit more difficult week in, week out. And the space given to all the off-road sport was being shrunk all the time under one off-road section, whereas when I joined the paper, much more space was given to speedway itself than the whole off-road section put together.

If I had been a 20-something, "going to make my own mark, going to change the world" kind of chap, I could have enjoyed the challenge more, but of course, I was over 50 and embarking on new, totally unchartered territory. I asked for and got early retirement.

Taking my pension early as a small lump sum and with money from my legacy from Mum and Dad's house when they died, I was able to buy a holiday cottage by the sea, which had a great view of the Norfolk coast, a county I grew to love. To pay the monthly bills, it was rented out as holiday accommodation, but Joy and I had some memorable holidays there, exploring a great part of the country, away from suburbia and motorway systems. I still lived in Northants, now in neighbouring Leicestershire.

To take early retirement and put the little pot of money into bricks and mortar was one of the best decisions I made.

It gave me another life, running a business outside of reporting on racing motorcycles, and it was a stiff learning curve, but I survived okay. I also bought a little flat with my pot of gold which I rented out; so that was another business to run, which for the most part went smoothly except for the occasional rogue who did a runner, once owing me nearly £1,000 in rent and damaging the property, so ongoing maintenance outlay kept going up.

One example. I put in new carpets, and Joy and I decorated the whole flat. When we returned, weeks later, the bathroom floor had been ruined with overflowing water, the new carpet had an iron burn mark in the corner, and there was mould growing everywhere because not a window had ever been opened! And the kid had crayoned on the wall. It broke our hearts. But you soon bounce back from life's little problems. I found long-term flat renting was not for me, and just kept on with holiday lets at the little Norfolk hideaway. Just great for those old-fashioned sun, sea, beach and walking holidays.

Chapter 31

In court!

To earn money, I got a job as a court reporter at Northampton Crown Court. Although as a young cub reporter with the *County Express* in Stourbridge, I had many years ago done my fair share of reporting magistrate court trials for the paper, that was the sum of my court experience. I did know court procedure and some basics about the law because it was one of the subjects covered in the National Union of Journalists one-day courses, which I attended (sometimes) in Birmingham for two years in those early days learning journalism.

But the Northampton Crown Court was a different type of court reporting altogether. Officially the title was court logger, and I was employed by a company who had a contract with the court service. Historically there had been shorthand writers who took down evidence like reporters. Now what a bunch of heroes they were, with their verbatim shorthand notes of such a quality that they were accepted as evidence right up to the highest courts in the land, and the government's *Hansard* record of parliamentary matters.

But they had been replaced many years before by tape recorder operators. Us. And I was in charge of a twin-deck tape recorder, sitting right under the judge and next to the court clerk, making sure that the proceedings of all trials were properly recorded on tape, listening, if need be, through headphones.

My job at the end of the day was to file these vital tapes away, along with hundreds and hundreds of other tapes, from all the courts for every day, every week. Working alongside my new colleagues who worked each day in the other courts in Northampton. If a case went to the Court of Appeal, my company could find my tape and have it transcribed as evidence, or sometimes when barristers wanted to listen to some evidence again to make sure they had got it right, or the defence was wrong, they came to us in the "court reporters" room, and we had to find the tape from the archived system for them to listen to. Sometimes the judges wanted to listen too, to make sure justice was done. At Northampton, we had a brilliant system in place, which 99.9 per cent of the time worked brilliantly through the head logger Mary's phenomenal skills.

Being almost centre stage during murder and rape trials and indecency cases, of which I listened to many, was hard to start with, but you just had to get on with it, and in the end, I enjoyed my 10 years of "court reporting". Some of the evidence in big trials, especially those involving children who had to give evidence behind screens right next to me, was harrowing and difficult to take, and we never received any hint of counselling. Somehow, in the end, you became used to hearing all this harrowing evidence, often with the accused people standing only a couple of feet away from you in the witness box.

But there was a happier, more social side to the job, and I met some very interesting and alarming characters along the way among the barristers, judges, court staff and other work colleagues at Northampton Crown Section, and when we were retired from this job, I did miss them all. Some friendships last to this day.

A tape malfunction on a machine during a trial was the worst thing to deal with because we had to tell the judge to stop the case because the tape had been "chewed up" by the machine and he would have to rise, often not best pleased. I was not as flamboyant as one of my colleagues, Genny, in this matter of stopping a trial. She used a walking stick to assist her, and when her tape stopped, her stick would fly into the air accompanied with a loud shout of "stop!" This happened a few times and, in the end, became part of the folk law at the Northampton Crown Court!

Court loggers are now a thing of the past, confined to history, dead as a dodo. We were all replaced by "automatic" digital recording of all courts and lost our jobs countrywide.

The breaks in trials were the best. With the public removed from the closed court, some barristers liked to tell a good story, and many were excellent gossipers and liked an audience. John Lloyd-Jones, later

Mr Lloyd-Jones QC, was one of the best storytellers, and we sat entranced many a time listening with others to law stories which will forever have to remain secret! Mr Lloyd-Jones, I met three years later in Market Harborough town, Leicestershire, and he said he trusted the judgement of ushers and court loggers in general of what the verdict of a case was going to be because they had sat impartially throughout proceedings and experience taught them how a case would resolve. Which, in general, I believe was true; you do get a feel for it when you concentrate your mind over several days of a trial. Much the same as a jury do when they are called to do their duty, as I once did.

It was 7 March 2012 when our jobs were finished. There was not going to be any trumpet blowing at our leaving, but wonderful (to us) Judge Richard Bray took it upon himself to hold a valedictory for the loggers at Northampton. Judge Bray addressed the loggers, this time we were all sitting in the jury box together: "Today is a special day in the history of this court, and it marks the end of the work of the loggers at this court, and I think at all the other Crown Courts in this country. Some of us remember when the loggers replaced the shorthand writers, and now they too have been replaced by a machine, something called DARTS. It is all part of the remorseless onset of technology. I understand that the Judges are soon to be replaced for sentencing purposes by a computer known as the GRID, short for Good Riddance to Independent Decision-making." That gives a small flavour of Judge Bray; some of the times, working in Judge Bray's courts could be very, very funny as he dished out justice in his own inimitable but fair way. There'll never be another. He too has retired. He said he was going to write a book on his days in court. Now that would be something absolutely amazing!

Judge Bray mentioned all of us loggers by name, saying of me, "Andrew does sports journalism and motorbike racing. He likes to walk up and down the court's concourse while waiting for court to start, or during adjournments, to get the flavour of defendants before they come in to court." But in reality, it was a case of exercise for me. I just had to walk around to get the circulation going after sitting down so long in some of the long court sessions, which you could not leave. Judge Bray concluded: "They (court loggers) have been part of our family here at this court, and we shall miss them very much."

Barrister Mr Lloyd-Jones then said: "I've been asked to deliver a reply written by Mary Gilbert, the Head Logger on her behalf and also on behalf of the other members of the departing logging team. Thank you, Judge Bray, for your kind words which are much appreciated. It is indeed a very sad and poignant day for us. If I were to mention everyone, I owe my grateful thanks to, we would be here all day and Judge Bray would undoubtedly be saying, 'Can we do some business here? (Meaning a guilty plea, before a trial was due to start), If not, can we please get on?' So, I will be brief. And so, we stand aside to make way for new technology, we thank you all for allowing us to be part of the family. We leave with heavy hearts but wish you all great success with the new technology. Thank you again, Judge Bray. We've done business, so let's get on."

It was an emotional day; one I will never forget. We were, in the main, treated with great kindness. And under our leader Mary, I think at Northampton, we did a great job for the courts, quite often in difficult circumstances. The ladies all received bouquets and the men, chocolates from the kindly court staff, who looked after us all so well. A story entitled "Judge's tribute as 'loggers' bow out" was reported in the next day's edition of the *Northampton Chronicle and Echo* by our reporter friend Rob.

Another book could be written on the goings-on behind a Crown Court, but I am sworn to secrecy! I've forgotten it all now, best thing. There must be something about courts and people in them losing certain body parts! It's not so bad, so read on, dear reader. Years before, when I worked for the *County Express*, a colleague and I were reporting on a coroner's court case, when suddenly he had to scramble with his hands on the table to retrieve his glass eye, which had fallen out and was bouncing about like a glass marble. At Northampton many years later, a barrister's tooth fell out during proceedings, and he asked for a recess and came back into court to Superglue it back in while seated on the front bench! Not before the general public, or jury I will add, just us court staff.

One thing and one thing only will I let out. A judge used to get little bits of paper passed to him during summer trials while he was sitting. Curious, I thought. But I got to know the secret. The judge was an avid cricket fan, and on the little bits of paper were the latest cricket Test match scores, handed quietly from the local court reporter via the usher!

Mr Lloyd-Jones QC, who spoke for the loggers on our final day, gave me a remarkable memory of one case. He was defending a man who would not recognise the court and stood in protest all through his trial. Mr Lloyd-Jones was given no instructions for his defence by the defendant, who remained mute at all times, although it was known he could speak. Still Mr Lloyd-Jones defended the man, looking out for his interests, and even managing to make a closing speech for his client. It was such an unusual case it still sticks in my mind and despite the impossible situation, Mr Lloyd-Jones did his best for his reluctant client, and the barrister received plaudits from the judge for his stoic efforts against all the odds.

On another occasion I recall a logger sitting in court all day, or perhaps all morning, completely forgetting to turn on the tape recorder. The person, shall we say, getting on in years, was not one of the regular team of loggers I must add, and the temporary forgetfulness of the person involved was quickly forgotten.

I can only remember one man escaping from the court. He took a dislike to his sentence and decided to jump out of the dock, not a secure one, and bolted through the door of the court, quickly followed by a member of the court staff, before running down the stairs and into the street for a brief stab at freedom, which did not last long as he was apprehended not long after. All he got was a longer sentence.

In my summing up of what I saw of justice and the law on the whole, it worked reasonably well, and as a system, it is the best we have come up with, after experiencing it for many years, first-hand. But behind the wigs and gowns, there are men and women who are highly trained and have completed years and years of study to be in a position to judge other men, but that is the strength and weakness of the law. They are only human and sometimes perhaps mistakes do happen, perhaps not during my watch, but there have been serious big cases involving miscarriages of justice that have been well reported. The law is a big stick, and just sometimes, the whack it gives can in my view be disproportionate. Rumpole, the fictitious barrister invented by John Mortimer, says he would not like to be a judge because who would want to try his fellow human beings anyway? It's a point, although delivered in a barrister's novel, but a point, nonetheless. Rumpole also says sometimes the case judgements and decisions handed down don't always bear scrutiny for all future time, and I think that statement should be remembered well.

Chapter 32

Speedway freelance years

To supplement my income from my court work, holiday cottage and flat, I set out to become a freelance speedway journalist. For a while I compiled the speedway league tables, results and fixtures for *MCN* which gave me money too, but that came to an end when they took even less interest in the sport.

The joy of my life was to compile weekly or monthly press releases on behalf of some of the world's top riders, and also press releases for two of the biggest clubs in the country, Wolverhampton and Coventry.

First on board was Simon Wigg! Simon was keen for me to help with his publicity, and for several seasons up to his enforced retirement, it worked admirably and superbly for us both.

Simon, one of the hardest working riders in the sport, was always abroad, racing somewhere, Germany or eastern Europe. Some of his trips were unbelievable, stamina-sapping exercises, but it was a way of life, a life on the road for Simon and his motorhome or van.

Simon would ring me on a Sunday night, sometimes really late while he drove back from a long track, grass track or speedway meeting, it could be Russia, Poland, Czech Republic, Estonia etc., telling me how he had got on. "Hi Andrew, I took the Bahn rekord (the fastest single lap of the track on the day), won the meeting, and I'm over the moon!" I'd write down all his news of the meeting as he or his mechanic drove back to the UK and then set to work to compile it as Simon's press release for that week. In those days, I sent the releases to all his main sponsors, newspapers, radio stations and people he was in contact with in Australia and all over the world, working through the agreed list of contacts and faxing them out individually on Simon's specially produced professional letter headings. I did each one individually, took me a long time, but was the only way I knew how to do it.

It worked a treat for many a season. Simon and I had a great working relationship, never had one falling-out, and Simon reached all those people he wanted to, especially valuable sponsors, keeping them bang up to date with all his racing successes, injuries, etc. I felt I was giving him a good service.

Some less professional riders than Simon were renowned for not paying for things and always had some excuse. Simon's little cheques were on the dot, every month and much appreciated. His local bike shop used to pin our little press release to the window so that the punters knew what Simon had been up to that week! I'd known Simon when I'd covered the sport at *MCN* but in the seasons I worked more closely with Simon preparing his press releases, I got to know him even better as a friend.

It became more difficult when Simon became ill, firstly through two epileptic fits in Australia when he lost his racing licence and his driving licence. But these were only pointers to the real trouble, and he underwent operations for a brain tumour.

He still wanted me to send out all this medical information to his sponsors and friends so that everyone would know the truth. The awful, mind-blowing illness was all related to me in the same professional manner as any of his great track successes, although he was naturally terrified of the outcome.

We even had a laugh during this immensely trying time – Simon discovered to his amusement he'd been reported in a Swiss motorcycle magazine as undergoing psychiatric treatment, which was, of course, not true! So, in it went in the press release quoting Simon as saying: "I'm still as mental as ever!" The last time I saw Simon was in a wheelchair at Coventry speedway. He said, "Hello, Andrew." I remember it well; the image is still burnt in my brain.

Unfortunately, Simon lost his battle for life and died in 2000, aged 40. His funeral on Monday, 27 November, generated a massive turnout at the Church of Christ the Cornerstone in Central Milton Keynes, with his immaculate racing bike at the centre of proceedings, which touched everyone. I remember Karl Maier, his great German long track rival, stopping everyone in their tracks with his moving eulogy to the late champ. All his family and friends were made welcome for refreshments at the National Hockey Stadium after the service.

After his passing, my life became much sadder. He touched my life and a good many more besides, mainly of course his wife, Charlie, and their too young children. Such a short life, but just look at the record he left behind, a record five-times World Long Track champion, World speedway runner-up, twice British speedway champion, six times British grass track champion. Nobody rode with more elegance and grace than Simon did. Another true motorcycling gentleman. A giant.

For years, the first Christmas card to pop through my post box is from his widow Charlie and her family. That means such a lot to me.

It was Simon who mentioned I was doing his press releases to Jason Crump, the enigmatic three times world champion Australian star, and he too became a client and a friend.

Jason was a little more difficult to get hold of some weekends than Simon. I reckon I've done the interview with him while he was soaking in the bath many times when he was in Sweden or elsewhere! But we got on fine and he too was pleased with the relationship we enjoyed; him giving me the information and me pumping it out via my overworked fax machine to all his sponsors, helpers, friends and people he wanted to be involved in his international racing team. A more professional professional you will never find. Stunning rider.

Jason does not suffer fools. But we were always straight with one another and our professionalism gelled well, and he knew one thing, I was not a fool. I had seen his dad race during his glorious British career and had become friends with Jason's grandfather, Neil Street, another extremely talented rider who was Australian team manager and a brilliant engineer. Neil started the new four-valve speedway engine revolution with his Street specials, based on the two-valve Jawa. Look where that went, right through to new Jawas, new Weslakes, new Goddens, all started off by the engineering brilliance of Neil and his engineering friends.

Neil and I still met occasionally after I'd left *MCN* at some GP I'd decided to go to for pleasure, and he was always glad to see me and tell me his news, always firing the information at you as quick as speech would allow! He was one of speedway's real gentleman and I was very sad when he died.

Also on board for my press releases was another Aussie, Steve Johnston. Johno was a real larger-than-life character, who always had a smile and a laugh with you, never seemed ever to get "down".

He produced his list of sponsors and supporters for me and I faxed his weekly press releases to them and that I think also helped him in his career, for he too took giving regular, informed press releases to his sponsors very seriously indeed, as did Simon and Jason.

I like to think that these press releases were informative and done with a little sense of humour to help portray these larger-than-life characters, especially Johno! Johno, the 1996 European grass track champion, also gave Sky Sport match commentaries, and his experience helped spot what most viewers would have missed had it not been for his expertise. I used to sort out with Steve all his racing fixtures in the UK, Sweden and sometimes Italy for the season and fax them all too, in one press release, so that everyone, his sponsors and supporters, knew where he was at any one time! As Steve's British career wound down, so did his need for my services, and it simply came to an end after I'd prepared his press releases for five or six years. A joker yes, but a top rider.

Next top man on board for my monthly press releases was Leigh Adams, another Australian and another great rider, who asked me to do the same service for him and his sponsors as I did with Wiggy, Jason and Johno.

We'd met up many, many times, starting when he was still riding in the world under-21 championships, first time maybe in Lonigo, Italy. Leigh's was an immense career and a more level-headed, straightforward man you'd never find. He was always ready for a chat with the press, and his comments were always worth listening to. In November 2000, Leigh wrote a lovely letter to me, signed personally on his Leigh Adams Racing headed notepaper.

He wrote: "Dear Andrew, thank you very much for your work throughout the season compiling my press releases. I appreciate you putting them together so quickly and fitting me in whenever I ring! You've done a grand job all season. I'll look forward to keeping our arrangement in place for next year, if you're keen. Best regards, Leigh."

Leigh is one of the sport's true gentlemen. I look back at our working together with great pride, as I do with Crumpy, Wiggy and Johno.

It was a tragedy that Leigh was so badly injured after his speedway career had ended, a career which had been largely injury free, only for him to crash practising for a desert race, which left him in a wheelchair. Once again, I was gutted for him and his family.

Joe Screen was also on board the Edwards' press release machine for a short time, and although I always got on very well with Joe during his career, from British Under 21 onwards, we never really got Team Joe Screen press releases going regularly. But we did try.

I kept up with speedway reporting by writing weekly press releases for a couple of seasons through my friendship with promoter Chris van Straaten at Wolverhampton and for Colin Pratt during his excellent tenure as promoter at Coventry. I sent out this PR work, detailing upcoming fixtures to the local newspaper editors, sponsors and so on, to keep them up to date with what was going on at the track on a weekly basis and to help those people who had not got a personal "ear" to Chris or Colin.

I also got an interview for the job as press officer for the British Speedway Promoters Association. I didn't get the job! It went instead to Nigel Pearson, who was younger, dynamic and had the right modern credentials with TV commentating (love him or hate him!) and computer literacy, much more qualified for the job than I, at my time of life.

I tried to help out the three-wheeler guys in 2001 in their quest to introduce the exciting speedway sidecars to tracks and give them a bigger professional profile. Sidecar speedway has always been a big part of racing on shale ovals Down Under, but never really took off in this country. Mainly because in the dim and distant past when sidecars had taken to the shale, they were just normal grass track outfits and were never intended to be ridden round tight speedway ovals, with their upright outfits and suspension for bumpy grass fields. They were spectacularly unspectacular!

But there was a new breed introduced in the new millennium, proper, specially built speedway sidecars, built with Aussie technology and which did indeed lend themselves to tight, exciting racing on our small ovals. They looked the part too with their all-enveloping state-of-the-art, colourful fairings.

I took on the role of press officer and did many releases to help out the Sidecar Speedway Promotions, run by former sidecar champions Paul Miller, Ken Lane and John Bailey.

The outfits they raced were very specialised pieces of kit with professionally built chassis, with no suspension, no brakes and highly tuned 1000cc engines from Yamaha, Honda and Suzuki. They pumped out 150–160bhp on speedway methanol – and boy did they go. They were built to go sideways, just like a solo, round the turns, as fast as could be envisaged, and they certainly were supremely spectacular. Racing was more often than not very competitive, and to see sometimes three faired outfits coming down the straight at full chat into a bend, with no one wanting to give way into the bend, had to be seen to be believed. Very entertaining stuff, as they bounced off each other's fairings to gain an extra six inches going into the turns!

The Super Cup had its own run alone series, just sidecars, with no solos in place. There was a qualifier at King's Lynn speedway in 2000, and the first full round was run successfully at Coventry stadium on 30 June 2001, followed by three more rounds at Poole, Isle of Wight and Workington.

The go-ahead promotion of Martin Ochiltree at Coventry had always had the speedway sidecars in the second halves of their meetings to give extra entertainment to the fans – are you listening promoters? – not 15 races and straight home, folks. That's it for this week!

The speedway sidecars were a success and ran into their second year attracting top Aussies to compete over here against their UK opponents. The opening round this time was at King's Lynn speedway where Aussies Darin Treloar/Justin Plaisted won from fellow countrymen Scott Christopher/Trent Koppe and third-placed Coventry pair Ivor Matthews/Tony Miles in the final.

Round two was at Workington, won with Treloar from Christopher, and it was the same result too at Coventry.

The organisers were to be congratulated on successfully getting an exciting new branch of the sport in front of crowds at UK speedway tracks, on a standalone basis. Some of the showmanship and spectacle of these sidecars would help make today's league match with no second-half meetings, more of a draw and more value for the spectator than is given today.

I compiled a page of Sidecar Speedway news, with much help from the promoters and Paul Miller, which was used weekly in *Speedway Star* with stunning action photos from Alan Whale. With more publicity, the British Sidecar Speedway championship was set up, and a few years later, one of the original aims of the Super Cup organisers came to fruition and took the sport into another phase when in 2006, the first FIM World Track Racing sidecar championship (Sidecar World Cup) was held at the Isle of Wight speedway, won by Scott Christopher and Trent Koppe. The Super Cup was held as a one-day event in 2008 also at the Isle of Wight, won by Darrin Treloar and Justin Plaisted.

Preparing press releases for the late, great Simon Wigg was one of my great pleasures. Always in my thoughts.

Chapter 33

Vintage speedway

In 1993, John Chaplin, who died in 2019, and Peter Lipscomb found a lovely niche for *Vintage Speedway Magazine,* which catered for those fans who had a passionate interest for the old days of early speedway history and published it four times a year for a glorious 10 years.

It was a quality magazine, and I was over the moon when John, on behalf of the magazine, asked me to be a regular contributor, with my own page, in the summer of 1999. John was a great speedway writer, out of the very top drawer of journalism and his insight, his knowledge and his wonderful books are legendary. When I was a youngster, John, with a wry smirk, always used to call me "Scoop!" which amused him.

I joined a wonderful line-up of columnists, including innovator Eric Linden, the *Speedway Echo* and *Speedway Star* editor, the "inimitable" Dave Lanning whose column inches in the *Sun* were a fantastic showcase for the sport for many years, the strictly "personal" Bob Radford, team manager, programme compiler, *Speedway Star* writer who had a wealth of knowledge on all things Scandinavian speedway, former *Speedway*

World editor Cyril J Hart, technical wizard Jeff Clews, Tony (Hawkeye) Hurren, Ivan Crozier, Ivan Mauger, Ove Fundin, Bert "Haggis" Harkins, Steve Magro and Peter Lipscomb himself, a master of memorabilia. "It adds up to probably the finest ever team assembled in speedway journalism under one banner," was the boast of John, himself a Fleet Street man and speedway author extraordinaire. We got some great interviews, said John Chaplin, including Ronnie Moore, but he thought the pinnacle was the one with Vic Duggan in his Australian home and the interview with Bluey Wilkinson's widow, Muriel. John and *Vintage Speedway* also got Peter Craven two British titles that the authorities didn't want to credit him with.

The magazine went worldwide, the cover price of £2 was never increased, and Peter did all the admin as joint publisher and John the editorial. Great days of which I was proud to be just a small part. Thank you, John and Peter. Issues are collectable now.

The magazine kept me busy finding out new comment on old stories, which kept the memory just a little sharper, although not at all times, and gave me a continuing link with speedway.

In the autumn issue 2002, which included a dramatic picture special and articles on The Death of Hyde Road, which had been for generations the most venerated of all tracks and the home of the greatest team of all, Belle Vue Aces in Manchester, I was able to give a twist to the tale, and the catalyst for the article had come from turning on the radio at 11.30pm and hearing unexpectedly on BBC Radio Four, the history of Belle Vue Zoological Gardens and Entertainment Park.

A Sense of Place told the story of Belle Vue through the ages, from its birth, its zoo, the funfair, with its scenic railway, with a brakeman standing up, giving a glorious view down onto the first bend of the Hyde Road track, its dance halls, wrestling, big bands, to the birth of rock and roll and disgraced Jimmy Savile's DJ Teen and Twenty show. And, oh yes, speedway did get a brief mention.

The mention was from a woman who lived just across the wall from Hyde Road who went to the speedway and met a man who became her husband, and who had a road bike. There was a poem too about Belle Vue that briefly mentioned the bikes "throttling round the track and the cinders flying into your eye."

What was interesting was the slice of social history that was Belle Vue. It was part of an age before annual holidays, when the highlight of the year for the majority of Manchester workers and their young families was a day trip to the great north-west leisure facility and its "roll up, roll up" shows, complete with elephants and tigers, conjuring up simpler, bygone days. There was probably a conjuror too.

It was a family day out and, of course, speedway, the family sport, fitted in really well with those other entertainments for years. It was a pity that speedway, an integral part of the story, was given such short shrift on radio and not a mention of one Belle Vue speedway rider's name, not even World Champions Peter Collins, Peter Craven, Ove Fundin and Ivan Mauger, all famous Aces, plus Jack Parker and the fact that the team were one of the best known and respected clubs in the country.

But the programme did mention that the sport was still active up the road at the Kirkmanshulme greyhound stadium, the original home of the Aces in 1928, a year before its move half a mile to Hyde Road. At least the painful end of Belle Vue's track in 1987 was not re-visited with its sale, and never forgiven by all true-blue speedway fans and enthusiasts worldwide, with its historic cups and trophies auctioned off like some old, dirty garden trousers.

I should not have been too upset at the lack of a few extra minutes being given to the story of the speedway on the Beeb, having had to endure like all speedway fans after the demise of Wembley was announced and the almost complete lack of any mention in the national press or TV of the Twin Towers championing the cause of the World Speedway Championship for all those decades of grandeur with so much elegance, we all remember of the Wembley Final nights.

What the late-night radio programme did do for me was to bring back memories of my first visits to Belle Vue; its famous wooden fence with no greyhound track to get in the way. Of superb, scary viewing for a youngster leaning over slightly, right up against the outside fence, for a face full of shale as the riders came flashing past just inches away at phenomenal speed. Shielding your face only with the flimsy, paper programme.

Or the view from one of its wooden stands, full for most of the time I went there in the 1960s for visits of Cradley Heath. And then one of my annual speedway treats, the British League Riders' Championship, which everyone knew in those heady days had a stronger in-depth field of riders than World Finals of the same era. Those magnificent meetings produced a heady atmosphere which most modern fans would die to have witnessed.

Another Belle Vue visit I remember was arranging a ride on Peter Collins's bike for the *Motor Cycle News* road test editor, Terry Snelling. Scary for Terry, of course, who never did quite forgive me for organising that little feature.

I can hear now the mighty exhaust of PC's bike reverberating in the empty stadium, opened specially for *MCN*, as he did some superb fast laps to show Terry how to slide a speedway bike, something completely alien to road bike testers. Terry bravely gave it his best shot and it helped *MCN* to another world exclusive, "We ride speedway ace Peter Collins' bike."

I also helped out filmmaker David Wood with centre-green interviews for PC's testimonial meeting at Belle Vue on Sunday, 29 March 1987, a bit of which survives in Roy Nicol's *The Collins Boys*, a superb video of the racing Collins family: Peter, Les, Neil, Phil and Steve.

But I never did take a ride on Belle Vue's scenic railway. Nor was I brave enough to get on PC's bike! Chicken eh!

Back in the *Vintage* magazine, Steve Magro recalled the night Christer Lofqvist made four-valve history in an issue in 1999 and I, or rather *MCN* got a nice little mention in the story too. Anders Michanek won the 1974 World Final in Ullevi Stadium, Gothenburg, Sweden (the first Final I reported on). Magro reported that Michanek said later: "They said Christer Lofqvist's special bike was better than anyone else's. I wanted to show that he and his engine were not as good as me." Christer's "four-valve special" however suffered problems, and he finished the meeting on a Jawa. Magro went on to tell the story of Christer (who died of a brain tumour in 1978) and his engine, which was a Swedish ERM (Endfors Racing Motor) with a tacho on the handlebars, which alerted me to the special machine.

Magro said: "Most reports of the 1974 World Final fail to mention its existence, though it was highlighted by *Motor Cycle News* in Britain." And that was written by me, keeping my eyes open for a "scoop". It must be said, of course, that it was the first four-valve engine only in the modern era, as pre-war Rudge machines had a four-valve engine. But JAPs were dominant by the time the world championships started in 1936.

I continued on my quest for speedway interests and knowledge, which took me back to Scandinavia in 2002, but this time for the first staging of a World Championship Grand Prix round in Hamar, Norway. It was an indoor meeting in a stadium shaped like an upturned Viking boat, and the temporary track was okay for racing. But the trip was memorable as well for a meeting, one of many during his lifetime, of one of my all-time favourite speedway characters, Neil Street, the former rider and Aussie team manager. I bumped first into grandson Jason Crump riding in the meeting and then Neil helping in the pits.

Being in Norway pricked Neil's memory banks and gave me another excellent article for the *Vintage Magazine*. Neil recounted a story of Norway in a different era when he had raced there not many years after World War Two. His particular adventure was with entrepreneur Trevor Redmond in charge, as were many in those days. Neil was part of an Australasian team which rode against a combined Norwegian-Swedish side in Oslo before going on to Sweden, Austria and Poland. It was 1957, Neil told me and with him were Redmond, Barry Briggs, Ronnie Moore, Jack Geran, Peter Moore, Jack Biggs, Peter Clarke and Aub Lawson. They sailed from Tilbury Docks to Gothenburg, Sweden, where they had two meetings and then Oslo, where they rode in the Bislett Olympic Stadium. The dirt running track was used after they'd filled in the water jump on the track with dirt. But it never compacted, and during the meeting it dug out and became a bit of a motocross type jump, which is difficult on a speedway machine, with no suspension.

Neil remembered a superb Norwegian rider called Basse Hveem, who rode before the war in Europe. He had been reserve for the 1952 World Final and rode briefly in the 1950s in England for West Ham. At the time of the tour, he was European Long Track champion and Scandinavian speedway champion. Basse had told Neil that during the war when Norway was invaded by the Germans, he buried all his JAP bikes and speedway equipment and dug them up after the war to use again.

After riding in Norway, the Australasian team drove back to Sweden for five more meetings, then on to Austria to race in Vienna, Linz and Gratz. A convoy set off to Poland through what was then Czechoslovakia. They got lost in a dreadful fog in Prague and ended up near the Austrian border again and had to wait several hours to get money to buy fuel for the vehicles. The riders were held up again at the Polish border, which was in those Cold War days guarded by machine guard posts, searchlights and 15–20 feet high barbed wire fences bordering half a mile of no man's land. They had money counted when they went into the country and when you left because you were not allowed to import foreign currency and not allowed to take Polish currency out either.

Having travelled all day, they got to Wroclaw after 5pm. The meeting had been planned to start at 2pm and the place was full of spectators. There were no protests though despite being kept waiting for three hours, and the riders could quickly see why. There was a ring of soldiers all round, complete with sub-machine guns. Being late in the year, it was so dark by heats seven or eight, the competitors could only see an outline of the rider in front and the sparks off his steel shoe, so the meeting had to be called off.

Everyone left the stadium without protest and no fuss because of the presence of the armed soldiers, said Neil. The riders went to a Polish banquet where they were served soup with raw eggs on top, which made them all feel queasy. The Poles had very little and were doing their best. Warsaw was an amazing sight. It had been completely decimated by the bombing, and Neil reflected that he thought there was only one service station open in the city for fuel. The tourists rode at five tracks in Poland, then turned round and had to face the journey all over again to get back home to the UK, said Neil. Now that's what you call a speedway tour!

Chapter 34

Programmes

I'd never been one for programme collecting, but it must be old age or something, as I've now become an "Ebuyer" and have got one programme, home and away, from each season of "my" team Cradley Heath who raced at Dudley Wood Stadium from 1947–52 and 1960–1995.

One of the most sought-after programmes is a one-off meeting in 1959 called the Cavalcade of Speed. At a local flea market near my home, a dealer was selling old programmes and, before I knew the value of this Cavalcade programme, I had it in my hand and for some reason put it back and I could have had it for 50p! The last one that came up for sale went for £130! You win some, you lose some. Anyone out there got one? I'll give you 50p!

My speedway for years was mainly Peterborough (nobody rides the Showground track like Jason Crump or Ryan Sullivan even now!), the new Leicester track and my favourite, King's Lynn (the Adrian Flux Arena). And to see National League Cradley Heathens at "Monmore Wood" for a few seasons.

The track at Saddlebow Road is always a credit to Buster Chapman and his family. It is well deserved that King's Lynn has been granted many big World Championship meetings over the years.

I like the racing at the Stars track and try to get there as many times as I can over a season, especially when I could watch the up-and-coming youngsters from Britain racing in the early National League matches, because King's Lynn supported that division with a team on a regular basis and I got to see the Dudley/Cradley Heathens racing against the Young Stars. With a Young Stars rider standing out in particular, one Robert Lambert. I saw him at 15 and quickly realised he would go far. So talented even then.

This is the class of racing that is most important in Britain, and only by more and more promoters running such youth-based programmes will Britain again attain anything like the international status it has lost over the years. It really upsets me because throughout most of my speedway reporting career I was able to write about and champion the sport, with Britain being at the top or near the top of ratings in World Team Cups, World Pairs and the World Finals themselves.

The top Premiership league became meaningless to me, with too many merely average foreigners in it for someone like me who reported on so much British success at World Championship, world cup and world pairs meetings and all the top riders in the world riding in Britain.

I am much more interested in the grass roots of speedway, the National League, and the British Youth Championship, where young British riders are given a proper chance. Unless these British riders are given the opportunity to ride in British teams, British speedway will never be the same and indeed might die altogether.

I love Buxton speedway. It is my favourite track. I love my visits there. The drive down the little, winding dale valley road is amazing and the first time you go, simply wonder, how can there be a speedway track down here? But there is, and I love it. No facilities to speak of, just a rusty metal container with the ref's box on top, rudimentary toilets, café, and that's it. But you can park your car next to the track, get a great view of the tiny track and an even more spectacular view over the Derbyshire countryside. And next to it, a hot rod track, all housed with no noise concerns in an old, disused quarry. Now that too is history.

Chapter 35

Characters along the way

My boyhood friends and I all pulled together in Stourbridge in 1971 to help build a Lotus Elan sports car from a kit of parts which were delivered on a low loader for Steve at his parents' house in Hanbury Hill. Can be completed in a weekend, the blurb yelled, but it took Steve Tromans, Gareth Morgan and John Vallender, next-door neighbours in Poplar Crescent, Norton, and I a full week to make sense of all those thousands of bits. Mind you, it didn't help the workshop manual for the Elan S4 arrived after we had built it! If you built it yourself, it was cheaper to buy, that's why we did it. And for the challenge, I suppose.

The *County Express*, Stourbridge, found it newsworthy for four local lads building a new car on a driveway for a page feature and photo of the completed car and new owner Steve.

We started, with help also from our friend Margaret Humphries, when she could, putting the chassis and body on four boxes. We found the car had been supplied with the wrong shock absorbers for a start which entailed dismantling and reassembly. "Offering up the diff" was the next thing we were told to achieve.

Four young men enveloped in the chassis pushed and pulled for two hours with no result in view. Steve recalled a tip to jack up the body and with this help, the diff finally was in place.

Half shafts are pretty simple. But not the Colin Chapman's Lotus patented rubber doughnuts. Fitting four bolts through each end was very time-consuming and the language became pretty profane. The engine, which thankfully came in one piece, went in quite well with a 12-foot hoist. But remember to fit the block and tackle before setting up the 12ft hoist because you can't reach it and when putting the engine in, remember to place the prop shaft in the tunnel. We were young and pretty green. That was when we found we had not offered up the manifold while the engine was put into place. So, it had to come part way out again.

One bracket for the radiator was fine, but one had the holes in the wrong place, so more drilling and cursing. When all was done, the little pretty Lotus fired up great. Unfortunately, the headlamp wire rubbed against the steering column shaft, producing interesting sparks on turning a corner and putting the lights out at the same time. Insulation tape was the answer to that. Steve worked out it took us about 45 hours to assemble, not bad without the handbook, I reckon.

The Lotus came to a sad end, however, in an accident, not the fault of Steve, it turned upside down with him hanging from the seatbelts. It was deemed a write-off.

One of my favourite cars was a sports car too, a tiny Fiat X19 in a lovely shade of green with a "Targa" roof which slotted under the front "boot" as it was a mid-engine car. Magnesium wheels were standard too, all for lightness, and it went round corners as if on rails with the engine fitted right behind your seat! I must like green, like Simon Wigg, as another car I had, another special one, was a Laser Green, Peugeot 205GTI, the quickest car I ever owned!

Steve, Gareth, John and I had many very happy holidays together before any of us were hitched to partners. One of Gareth's friends lent us a small, old caravan in Wiseman's Bridge on the Pembrokeshire coast. Idyllic. Except on Sunday, we found the local pub shut. We hadn't taken into account the Welsh Sunday licensing hours. But the adjoining shop was happy to slip us bottles of beer under the counter in brown paper bags as they weren't allowed to sell alcohol either. I believe we found the pub was actually "open" on a Sunday as well, indeed busier than ever, you just had to know to go in through the back door and drink with the locals including, I fancy, the local plod.

Steve got a bit tiddly shall we say one night in the pub, drinking stuff he had never had before. There was a Welsh rugby club singsong as well, I seem to recall, and a rollocking night was had by all. But Steve said he was hungry when we got back to the caravan and insisted on making bramble jelly sandwiches, which we all told him was a bad mistake, which it was, and he added an interesting shade to the caravan side as he stuck his head out of the window... I never got drunk again in my life, said Steve.

I had my Austin A30 then, John a Mini with a 1300cc engine in it, Steve a Morris 1000 and Gareth a Triumph Herald, which he wrote off in an argument with a large curb with all of us on board sometime later. All vehicles seemed to go to Wiseman's Bridge, I believe, because we all ended up going on different days or had to get back at different times for work.

Steve, John and I all played at the local badminton club, and Gareth always joined us for a drink and a game of snooker afterwards in the Stourbridge Institute. We all were Cradley speedway fans too, but I don't think Steve went all that often.

We had a lifetime of friendship although, of course, we all went our separate ways with marriages and relationships, from teenage years to middle and older age. Less contact, but always in one another's thoughts. Gareth happiest when he ran his own car body repair shop, rock and roll dancing, or fishing, Steve with his own optician businesses, always owning an interesting car, gardening, getting a suntan on his "hot" holidays, John a high-flier council executive who loved Greece and spent time there with his wife and family. Unfortunately, Gareth and John have passed over. We were the greatest of mates. Great days, growing up together, knowing one another's secrets, having a good time, saw happy times and sad. Halcyon days, never to be forgotten. Relationships which endured, never completely losing touch. Yes, and they were all interesting, wise and lovely characters to spend time with as it is with best friends, never an argument or fallout from any of us.

Another great character I met along the way a few years later was Bill Ojala. We met because we were seated next to one another on the London plane bound for Gothenburg, Sweden, where I was going to report on a World Final for *Motor Cycle News* 1974.

I found him an interesting American from California and ticked all the boxes as a, shall we say, quite loud American. He said he didn't have a room, and I took a chance and said he could kip on the floor in my room if he had nothing else. This he was quite happy to do, and we got on really well. Bill loved his speedway, and I believe had several machines, one of which was in his lounge at home.

We kept in touch by email for several years when the chance came for him to come to Rockingham Speedway, not our shale sport, but the full tarmac oval variety so loved in America and which was then open for business in Corby, Northants, near my own home. Bill knew one of the British drivers who he'd met in America and wanted to meet up with him again too.

Bill rang me and said why not meet him in London where he was going to stay on a boat in the Thames belonging to controversial artist Damien Hurst. I didn't go for some reason. He was "Uncle Bill" to Damien, who was married to Bill's niece. "You can have the car and Keith (Damien's chauffeur) will drive for you for the weekend," said Damien.

We arranged for him to come up to Northants for the weekend, and Bill said that he'd see us at the home of my partner, Joy, where he would be put up for the night before the Rockingham races. He came with Keith the chauffeur and a lovely Audi A8 car and put it on Joy's drive.

We had a lovely meal at the local pub restaurant where I remember everyone turning round when Bill laughed because he was pretty loud. I don't think he ate one vegetable on his plate that night, just the steak.

We had a hilarious time trying to inflate a bed after we'd been down the pub, and if memory serves me, we were all trying to blow down the wrong end after the electric motor didn't seem to be doing anything!

We had a superb day out at Rockingham watching the car racing with Bill and we had a great time as guests in the pits. Years later, he did find me again on Facebook.

Brian Griffin, I came across through my association with Simon Wigg and his grass track and long track exploits as Brian was a big sponsor, promoter and friend of Wiggy. We used to meet up at British grass tracks and long tracks in Germany and the Czech Republic. He sponsored Simon for a couple of years, including 1989, Simon's best ever year when he was British grass track champion, British speedway champion, world speedway runner-up and world long track champion. But Brian had the same background as me, he was born in Lye, near Stourbridge in the West Midlands, properly named the Black Country, while I was born in Amblecote, a mile or two from Lye. He had aspirations to become a speedway rider apparently but was not supported by his parents. We both attended those early days at Cradley Heath speedway. And if my recollection is correct, for a short time, many years later, thought of promoting the club but was put off by the restraints the speedway authorities put on owners. He did follow his dream later on and was co-promoter of King's Lynn speedway club with Mike Western in 1999, taking over from Buster Chapman, in 2000 the promoting team was Brian, Nigel Wagstaff and Buster, and in 2001 it was Brian and Wagstaff. Then he chose to call it a day.

But Brian's profession is that of one of the world's leading photographers, practically royalty! As well as outstanding achievements in commercials and the music industry. Hundreds of portraits of pop stars, leading actors and artists of the day and many iconic album covers have all been charismatically captured by the lens of Brian in an epic career.

His photograph on the album cover of Depeche Mode's *A Broken Frame* is described by Wikipedia as "often cited as one of the best colour photographs ever shot." The same photo was used on a supplement cover of *Life* magazine's best photos of the 1980s. On top of that, Brian was named by the *Guardian* newspaper in 1989 as the photographer of the decade.

Brian is based in London but has an even greater reputation abroad, especially France, is an Honorary Doctorate of Birmingham University and his work sits in the Victoria and Albert Museum and the National Portrait Gallery, London.

Brian could have been included in a series MCN ran for several years, called Superfans, and I was able to contribute a couple from speedway.

At six feet tall, you could not miss Sam "Top Hat" Messer, a Cradley Heath fan through and through. The hat was in the Heathens colours of green and white, topped with speedway badges. My recollection is that he wore a suit with a badge bar on the lapel. He had an extremely loud Black Country voice did Sam, and he led the army of Cradley supporters with their war cries home and away, many years before the barmy army of English cricket fame – Cradley had their own hard core in the 60s and 70s.

He never had a go at speedway because he knew he would be too mad, he told me.

But he did help behind the scenes at the club where he helped run training schools, often driving the grading tractor. He carried Cradley's world runner-up Bernie Persson round the greyhound track on his shoulders after his success at Wembley in 1972! No mean feat that.

Another Superfan was a Leicester fan known as "Derek Minter", which was not his real name but that of his hero Derek Minter, the ace British road racer. "Derek", the Lions and Ray Wilson fan, was a regular at the Blackbird Road track and had the late Derek Minter's bike tattooed on his arm in the early 60s, and I included Derek – real name Ken Haywood – in *MCN*'s series The Motor Cycling Superfans in November 1973.

Ken wasn't keen on tattoos, but his mates egged him on, so he said he'd have Minter's famous "Thunderball" Norton inked on his arm.

Ken was a great supporter of Mallory Park racetrack and, after nearly 40 years, I was at Mallory for a bike meeting when I ran into Ken in the paddock. We both recognised one another instantly, and I managed to send him a copy of the *MCN* article in which he starred as a Superfan as I was able to find an original for him.

On a Leicester Lions Blackbird Road visit, you were bound to see a larger-than-life character called "Soldier Boy", nicknamed presumably because he had been in the army. But you didn't as much see "Soldier Boy" as hear him. He had a voice like a foghorn and used to get so carried away shouting that his face would turn purple!

He had his own heroes, which over the years included Ray Wilson, the Lions number one, Peter Collins and Malcolm Simmons. But having him on your side was a mixed blessing. He was not averse to giving criticism of "his" rider when he thought they needed it and it was delivered at the top of his voice, shouting over the pit fence. I think the riders took the outspoken comments in their stride, although sometimes, it must have been difficult!

I met another colourful character in 1992 during the ICE (International Championship Events) indoor ice speedway series in Tucson, Arizona. *MCN* had got a free trip to publicise this non-FIM affiliated event which had attracted British riders Martin Dixon, Mark Crang, Marcus Bisson and Dave Roberts. It was held in January and so was good for copy as events to report on were in short supply during the winter months.

The character was Johnny Griffits, a Vietnam Veteran, then 44, who not only sang, and sang well, the "Stars and Stripes", the USA's national anthem before the ice event, but rode his own creation, a one-off speedway bike that I'd never seen before, a Harley-Davidson. Johnny was sponsored by Harley-Davidson of Tucson, and the bike he'd built was one half of a Harley V-twin, which made it 500cc single!

I spent several days hanging out at the Harley Tucson "shop" watching Dixon and others prepare their bikes and stud the tyres for the upcoming event and talking to the Harley owners. I was in heaven. All sorts of Harley types came into the dealers for their bits and pieces. There were three types of silencers for the road bikes, the dealer said, one legal, one loud and one that will definitely get you stopped by the police!

But back to Griffits. His bike was professionally built and looked good in its proper speedway frame, but it never performed that well on the ice because electrical problems stopped the engine running well. I don't think for one minute that it would have kept up with the GM, Weslake, Godden, Jawa specialised equipment, which was used by everyone else, but it was a great effort of originality which made a nice feature in *MCN*. Being American, the Harley and Johnny were greeted by a good cheer as he came out for each of his races when patriotism kicked in. It was in Tucson that I saw how serious Americans were about their national anthem when a guy near me forgot to take off his baseball cap while the anthem was being played, and the cap was quickly tipped off his head by an irate countryman!

I also managed a quick trip to Mexico to the border town of Tijuana, which became another country I could tick that I had seen!

Vietnam veteran Johnny Griffits in Tucson for the indoor
ice with his Harley-Davidson 500cc single, he manufactured
from a 1000cc V-twin! He sang the national anthem before
the meeting too. Brilliantly!

The border town of Tijuana, just south of California, was as
far as I got in Mexico while at the LA World Final and again
later for the Indoor Speedway Finals.

The third World Championship held in the TCC Arena, Tucson, was totally unofficial but provided plenty of spectacle with two divisions, solo speedway bikes and quads. It has to be said it was more along the lines of Ian Thomas and Graham Drury's fun one-off winter ice racing in Telford, Shropshire, rather than the wicked world ice speedway championship seen at places like Assen in Holland and in Russia, but nonetheless, still a fix for the fans.

An article I wrote in *MCN* in 1995 featuring sidecar grass track champion Gary Jackson had a surprising, embarrassing consequence for me! The article described Gary's high-tech 1000cc Yamaha EXUP-engined outfit, which the clever engineer rider had turned into a "big bang" engine, the same technology employed in the V4 500 GP engines. Gary would only say the firing order was changed, which you could tell because instead of the high-pitched wail from the high-revving EXUP, the Jackson jet throbbed like an old-fashioned twin. He had two cylinders firing at a time, we guessed. To change the firing order of an EXUP was a major job requiring a completely redesigned crankshaft and major changes to the ignition, all done by Gary himself. The idea behind the brilliant home-built technology was to cut wheelspin and add traction to the Yamaha. It worked brilliantly and when on form he was virtually unbeatable on the wonderful machine.

But in the story, I called Gary "a big, ruddy-faced man who looks more like an 18th-century blacksmith than a master of high-tech machinery."

He got me! Sidecar ace Gary Jackson presented me
with a surprise horseshoe at a grass track.

Later that season, I was reporting on a big grass
track meeting when the track announcer called me up
on the presentation stage at the end of the meeting,
where stood Gary Jackson. He had a surprise for me,
and I had my comeuppance, as they say. In front of the
crowd, he presented me with a big horseshoe because
in the article I'd said he looked like a blacksmith! It
was all good fun and I still have the horseshoe!

I was always told by *MCN*'s Norrie Whyte to dress
smartly when travelling by plane and ask airlines if
an upgrade was on offer. They would never give an
upgrade to the first-class cabin to someone dressed in
t-shirt and jeans. Coming back from this event, for the
one and only time in my life, it paid off and I travelled
back from Chicago to Britain in a first-class seat, with

proper metal knives and forks with which to eat meals and big seats with plenty of space. Heaven.

On the journey out, we'd landed at Houston airport and several passengers' bags, including mine, had gone on to Las Vegas. So, I've always said, I've never been to Vegas, but my luggage has! We had a couple of days living from a tiny toilet bag with toothbrush, soap etc., care of Continental airlines, before our bags were retrieved after their visit to the gambling capital.

The little Channel Island of Alderney became a favourite holiday haunt for me for several years, and it was there in that unusual backwater I found Glyn Chandler a Cradley Heath rider from the 60s, who was an island resident. So that led to a speedway feature too.

Glyn had ridden from 1955 for Ringwood and Eastbourne before being selected into his home Swindon team in 1956, followed by spells at Neath (1962), St Austell the following year, then Cradley. He rode right up until around 1970 (that year for Long Eaton Rangers in Division Two) and in 1976 went to live in the idyllic Channel Island.

Glyn still had old speedway bikes and still took part in veteran races. I photographed him wearing his CH body colour sitting on a vintage BSA.

Glyn was into vintage bikes and had several which he had beautifully restored, and which were regularly used on the island by him and his wife, Sally, who rode a restored 1956 Royal Enfield.

We had a lovely day talking old speedway times and taking pictures of him sat on his 1925 BSA while wearing his original green and white CH bib from 1964. Sadly, Glyn died in 2014.

One of the most unusual old speedway bikes I've ever come across was on display in Rothwell Heritage Centre, just a couple of miles from my home. I'd never seen one like it before and the bike went back to nearly the start of the sport in this country. It was an original bike from a 1937 fairground ride called the Ark.

The bike was one of 54 made by Orton & Spooner for the Ark ride that was new in 1937. It was made of wood with the graphics of a bike with an engine and wheels, with a wooden handlebar and leather seat. It sounds by its history the bike has had a long and varied use.

In 1948 the whole fairground ride "speedway bikes" was sold to J Fletcher. And eight years later it was sold on to Hall Brothers in 1956. In 1957, still with the bikes on it, instead of the traditional fairground horse rides, it passed to Ernest Atha, who had the ride for 28 years. It is best known under that name, and there was a photo of the ride in Atha's name at the centre. It was sold to Herbert Hirst in 1985. Many bikes have Hirst on their number plates. The caption said the ride was now a waltzer and was owned by James Hudson. Quite an extraordinary piece of speedway history and shows how mainstream speedway was for a fairground ride to be centred around the sport.

Chapter 36

Mum's book

IF you are reading this book, it means I have managed to have it published to tell my own story.

But many, many years earlier, my mum, Mary, had written her own family story.

Mum's book was never published, although all members of the family have a copy of the typed manuscript. She tried so hard to get it published, but it was not in a style that could be used as a book. Mum was devastated that all her hard work had come to nothing.

At home in "Burwood", Amblecote, West Midlands, with, from left, back row: me, my dad and Joy. Front row, Cassie, my mum and Vicki, September 1994.

Her book WAS hard work, hard labour for her. She had no formal further education, just had the basic "three Rs" at school. But, for this book, she learnt how to type with one finger on an ancient portable typewriter and set about telling us all her memories of a childhood, written in her own inimitable style. She suffered much ill health and was housebound for many years, so this typing was a labour of love and took months to achieve. Now this is hard to believe but is true. She did not know about carbon paper, where you can make a copy of each page you type. When she had finished typing her book, she began putting another sheet of paper in the typewriter to type it out again! She did at least four copies! Incredible, unbelievable. I did get her some carbon paper, but only later! My mum was not to be beaten and tried her best to publish her story. What a woman. I wish I had helped her more with a major project of her later life, but because I was so busy with *MCN*, I didn't, and I regret it.

But although she never got her book published, I will now put in print for the first time the title she gave to that typed document, typed with all her passion and determination, against all the odds. She called it *One Speck of Ordinary Black Country Ash*.

It was not a speck at all; she wrote 30 chapters which ran to 94 typed pages! Here is the end of the book, written as she typed it.

"I look forward to a lunch date unexpectedly with our son, or my hubby, for an hour. Evenings with the sunlight in the trees, bringing lengthening shadows onto lawns.

"The stillness and silence of late evenings in the Far Forest" (near Bewdley, where my parents had an old caravan, her bolt hole, her sanctuary).

"A special treat too, is in managing a run in the car, often still in around the Midlands, remembering the early days when we were cyclists, and ardent ones at that, over the same roads.

"We still can get off the well-known roads, using some of the smaller lanes, of our 'heyday'. Able to stop and stare at the beauty spots in and around our locality.

"Then twice a year, a longer, steady run to near seaside's, where I now just absorb the views. We find the smaller places in Wales suit us.

"It is very awesome to stand alone, generally late at night and watch the ebbing and flowing of the sea. To stand looking across at the huge stretch of water, wave after consistent wave, one cannot but realise one's own smallness in this universe. One tiny drop in a big ocean. Each and all having to put into life, to get anything out of it. Helping the stream of life along.

"Or should I say, hoping one day, just to be ONE ORDINARY SPECK OF BLACK COUNTRY ASH."

There, you made it, Mum, you've been published.

Chapter 37

The biggest laugh

Always leave everyone with a laugh and a joke say the old comedians, like Ken Dodd when he entertained me and a hundred others in the bar at the Castle Mona Hotel, Douglas, Isle of Man, all those years ago.

But this is my own way of leaving with a laugh and a joke. And I believe all the participants did eventually forgive me and see the joke for what it was.

I always read the April Fool's jokes in the daily national papers, a story which purported to be a real news story but was a made-up load of old twaddle by journalists. I wondered if I could do an April Fool's joke in *MCN*. It was coming up to April 1, and a lot of newspapers did an April Fool's joke story then. Even the BBC got a great spoof in one year with footage of spaghetti growing on trees! Wonderful.

I started to get the germ of an idea and got the go-ahead from my editor to use it as the lead story in my Speedway page, due to be published on April 1. The story was that Oxford Cheetahs had signed a young, American speedway woman champion from California and were to ride her alongside club number one Hans

Nielsen against Cradley Heath, who were to be their next opposition.

I phoned Oxford promoter, the late Bernard Crapper, with my idea. He was larger than life, always up for a good laugh, and liked my devious plan. One of his own stories he told was how as a Freeman of the city of Oxford, he was allowed to fish off all the bridges in the city. Maybe true for all I know!

But back to my jape. Bernard had a quirky sense of fun and was up for it when I told him what I was about to do, so we got out a press release between us. Bernard, bless him, never even told his own press officer Glyn Shailes, who quizzed him on the story. "Where's she going to change?" asked Glyn.

"In my office," said a serious Bernard. On it went. The story was published in *MCN* saying that the lady in question was to ride for Oxford in heat one alongside Hans in the Oxford v Cradley match.

This is what went in as the lead story on the speedway pages that week.

Headline: "Debbie to destroy girls ban."

"British League champions Oxford Cheetahs have become the first team to sign a girl rider – and she will be riding alongside Hans Nielsen in their League Cup encounter.

Under Speedway Control Board regulations, women are specifically banned from racing in this country, but Cheetahs go-ahead promoter Bernard Crapper is set to take on the sport's governing body and he reckons he'll win any court case right up to High Court level.

So today he's signed 21-year-old blond Californian racer Debbie Cherber who has been impressive in behind closed doors training sessions at Cowley.

"She's the best girl prospect I've ever seen and with her undoubted enthusiasm and skill I reckon she can be the first woman speedway champion in four years' time" said a delighted Mr Crapper.

Busty Miss Cherbar who breasts the tape at 38–24–36, will form the first man/woman opening pair in the world with Nielsen.

"The authorities may think they can stop me, but not this time. We have the Sex Equality Act on our side and I am looking forward to playing a decisive role," said Mr Crapper.

"I have cleared it with the rest of the team and they are not bothered by showering with Debbie, in fact, they are quite looking forward to the first meeting."

The British Speedway Promoters' Association and the Speedway Control Board were tight lipped about the situation."

At that time, Peter York, a good friend of mine, was manager of the British Speedway Promoters' Association. His phone was red hot that morning with calls from several promoters in the BSPA. One such call was from Colin Pratt, the Cradley promoter, who resolutely stated he was not taking his team to ride against a team with a woman in it.

Listening and learning from Colin Pratt, left, one of speedway's most influential personalities, ex-rider, team manager, club and international level, and promoter. Diamond bloke.

It was against the rules laid down by the sport, he said. The BSPA manager got on to Bernard, telling him that his phone had been constantly ringing since early morning because of a newspaper story in *MCN*. What was going on, said Peter, what was Bernard trying to do to him. You can't sign a woman and put her in an official match, Peter argued.

"Oh yes I can," said Bernard, trying very hard not to laugh. The conversation went on and on, and Bernard was steadfast that a woman, Debbie Cherbar, was going to ride in his next match at Cowley Stadium, and nobody was going to stop him. She was racing in heat one with Hans Nielsen as her partner. "I've done the deal. She will ride," said Bernard.

In the end, Bernard relented with poor Peter and said, "Stop, stop, Peter, what is the date today, what is the date? Look it up." There was silence, followed by, "You b***dy bu**er." And the phone was slammed down. Colin, a good friend of mine, didn't speak to me for a couple of weeks when I went to Cradley, but he forgave me in the end, and he is a very dear friend.

Peter, the ultimate professional, also saw the funny side of the story, eventually! Re-reading the story, published in 1992, I can't believe how sexist the story I wrote was. How times change in over 20 years! But I think the warning signs were there for anyone reading between the lines... The story has taken on a life of its own. A vintage speedway magazine years later mentioned the story of the mysterious woman speedway rider. And I had to explain it again. That was the day Oxford speedway "signed" a woman speedway rider.

Speedway and journalism gave me a great life. Keep speedway's flag flying! (And *MCN*'s too!) I loved it all.

About the author

Andrew Edwards is a journalist, self-employed freelance writer and PRO for many speedway riders, plus Wolverhampton and Coventry speedway and Sidecar Speedway. He was employed by the *County Express*, Stourbridge, West Midlands, and *Motor Cycle News*. He contributed to many titles including *Speedway Star*; *Classic Bike*; *On Two Wheels*; *Ivan Mauger's Extravaganza*; *Motorcycle Year 1976–77*; *Vintage Speedway Magazine*; and *Hindsight: The Journal of Northamptonshire Association of Local History*.